Tokyo

TOPOGRAPHICS

Tokyo
A View of the City

Donald Richie

with photographs by Joel Sackett

REAKTION BOOKS

for Edward Seidensticker

Published by Reaktion Books Ltd
11 Rathbone Place, London W1P 1DE

First published 1999

Printed and bound in Great Britain by
Biddles Limited, Guildford and King's Lynn

A catalogue record is available from the British Library.

ISBN 1 86189 034 6

Whether Armilla is like this because it is unfinished or because it has been demolished, whether the cause is some enchantment, or only a whim I do not know...

ITALO CALVINO

I have lived in Tokyo now for over 50 years, yet I have not come to take it for granted as many people do the places they live in. One of the reasons is that since I remain an alien – as do all foreigners who live in Japan, even those who live here for half a century – I perforce see myself as separate. Always the exception, I see everything as exceptional.

Another reason is that I was born in a small town in rural Ohio, and – despite having lived most of my life in Tokyo, among the largest cities in the world – I have never gotten used to vast urban spaces. Big cities remain something to marvel at, to worry about and to admire – not to take for granted.

Yet another reason for a resident's remaining so conscious of Tokyo is the city itself. It is unlike any Western capital, is built differently and is used differently. Even reconstructing it on paper, which is what this book is meant to do, calls for special means of presentation.

Certainly, to have offered a logical, straightforward, obvious historical description of the place would have been to misrepresent this illogical, subtle, brash, teeming and utterly human place. Therefore, I decided to draw my picture of Tokyo in the shape of Tokyo itself. Thus I start with the core. Edo Castle (now the Imperial Palace) is the core in a double sense, both spatially and temporally. From this beginning, we walk along the still-circular streets that surround this core, writing of developments. As the circles become more irregular, we stray to related topics, led (as is the city) by association, and by the end of the book we are out in the suburbs.

This is perhaps not the ordinary way to construct a book, but Tokyo is not an ordinary city, and through this construction I hope to reflect the sudden turns, the instant felicities, the surprising incongruities of the place. And I can also, I hope, show something of what being here is like.

Donald Richie
Tokyo, 1999

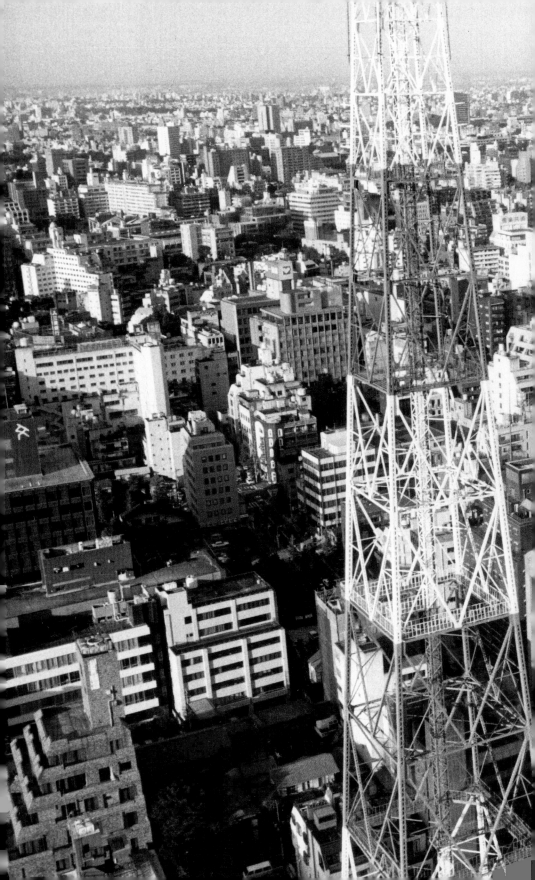

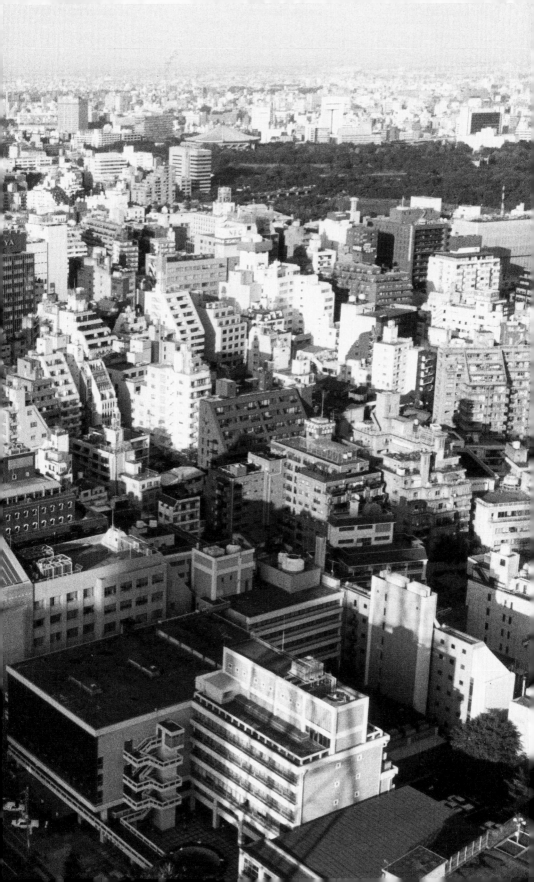

Tokyo: a view of the city

Many cities have individual styles. Venice, Bruges, Amsterdam, Rome, Paris – each has a style that is particular to it. Other cities do not. In Tokyo, one feels – as Henry James felt of London – that the city has no single style, only innumerable attempts at style.

Some of the attempts are attractive (Grosvenor Square, the Imperial Plaza), but there is no overriding conception. One of Tokyo's reasons for such a lack is that while some cities (New York, Rome, Istanbul) are still knit together by remains of their pasts, Tokyo has very few of these.

What with fires, earthquakes and massive aerial attacks, the city has long been accustomed to being burnt down and built up, and though the invariable traditional construction materials – wood, roof tile – gave a certain sense of uniformity, Tokyo has few historical buildings and hence lacks a basis for anything so uniform as a style.

Almost nothing of Edo – as the place was called until 1868 – remains, except the bare grid of the original streets. The buildings along these are all relatively recent and relatively Western in pattern. As they progress towards the present, the city comes to look new, raw, unfinished. The past style (what there was of it) is no longer visible, and the present style is no style at all.

One might say, then, that Tokyo's style is an absence of style – that is, there seems to be no overriding authority (which is what style is – a kind of government) – and that the resulting mayhem *is* the style of Tokyo. One feels about it as Alexander Payne said he felt about London in 1872: 'Nothing is more striking . . . than the utter confusion and want of plan to the place.'

It was sheer size that saved London and prompted Dr Johnson to speak of its 'wonderful immensity' and for Henry James to echo him a century later with the observation that '. . . the mere immensity of the place is large part of its merit.' It is this which saves Tokyo as well.

Within a 50-kilometre radius of the Imperial Palace live 27 million people, some three million more than in all of California. Tokyo is large and growing still. Yet not half of this population is native; they have come from other sections of the country, and more come all the time. They always have. Even back in Edo times there was a saying that the city consisted of 'drifters from every province'.

The place has also long been overcrowded. Space is costly anywhere in Japan, but in the capital it is especially expensive. No-one here can hope any longer to own their own home, and flats are expensive and small. Paul Waley, writing of the 'receptacle nature' of Tokyo, speaks of the 'pencil buildings, eight-to-ten story, wobbly, windy structures that afford room only for hole-in-the-wall offices and apartments'. Shops, bars, restaurants are fitted into stray corners of the city; places seating only six or eight are stacked one on top of the other like serving plates. A stall in a capsule hotel just fits the horizontal human body, and television is viewed between the feet.

Tokyo is famously a city where rush-hour pushers are employed to shove passengers into already packed trains, where losing a shoe in the scramble is not uncommon, where a crowd of a million (one place, one time – New Year's at Meiji Shrine) is ordinary. It is also a city where the sheer number of people to stare at can be exhilarating. As Constantin Guys (quoted by Baudelaire, as quoted by Walter Benjamin) said: 'Anyone who is capable of being bored in a crowd is a blockhead.'

An enormous city, Tokyo writes all of its qualities huge. One can see the same confusion and want of plan in a number of small Japanese cities, but they have nothing of the expression they achieve in Tokyo. Indeed, the enormous lack of standardized streets, of stereotyped structures, creates its own kind of effect. With its vast lack of an apparent plan, its mammoth deficiency of any civic attention, the place appears profuse, febrile, prodigal and extravagant – at least compared to such planned places as Beijing and Washington, D.C.

It was like this early on. The amazed Dr Philipp Franz von Seibold exclaimed in 1823: 'I can compare the bustle of Edo to nothing but that of London.' And Tokyo still gives the impression of burgeoning life absolutely everywhere – flourishing in channels it is true, but burgeoning none the less.

This is a quality one associates more with Asian than with Western cities, and indeed Tokyo is much like Calcutta with all the amenities, or Singapore before the city planners wrecked it. Japan's capital retains the enormous size of its population. It is in this sense an intensely human city.

One need not feel about it as Shelley felt of his capital: 'Hell is a city much like London . . .' One may rather feel about Tokyo as James felt about London – that it was 'the particular spot in the world which communicates the greatest sense of life'.

Though Japanese municipalities, particularly Tokyo, may appear to be reassuringly, or distressingly, Western, even a short acquaintance with these modern-seeming cities indicates that they are not Western nor, indeed, in any Western sense, modern.

The high-rise structures, the elevated highway networks, the proliferating suburbs are sights familiar to the West, but the city functions in an un-Western manner. Tokyo may look like Dallas-Fort Worth, but it does not act like it.

Roland Barthes noted that reticulated cities (Los Angeles is his example) produce an uneasiness because '. . . they offend our synesthetic sentiment of the city.' This sentiment requires that any urban space have a centre to go to and return from.

Tokyo may have a centre (the Imperial Palace and its grounds), but that centre is empty. 'The entire city,' Barthes continues, 'turns around a site both forbidden and indifferent.' It is indeed built around a central emptiness that forces traffic to make a perpetual detour.

Another indication of difference occurs when Western visitors attempt to locate an address. Their assumptions are that a city is planned, that there is a logic to be discerned in its structure. Empty-cored Tokyo, however, initially exhibits nothing of the sort.

Many of the streets are not named, though most of the crossings are. The plots along these streets are not numbered, though the houses are. But even if the districts are numbered, the order is often

13

arbitrary (sometimes still based merely upon seniority of construction) and varies, ward by ward.

As Edward Seidensticker, the pre-eminent historian of Tokyo, puts it, '. . . the consciousness of place continues to be by tract or expanse and not by line.' The actual finding of an address 'is a matter of navigating in more or less the right direction, and asking aid and comfort upon approaching the bourne'. Thus, here as elsewhere in Japan, the civic concern which Westerners are accustomed to in their own cities, the assumption that a private address is a public matter, seems to be missing.

There is indeed little civic convenience of the architectural sort taken for granted in the West. Given the size of Tokyo, there are few large central parks and no real congregation of cultural facilities. In 1986, on his first helicopter ride over Tokyo, the poet Anthony Thwaite noticed 'for many miles on every side . . . a dense sprawling huddle of smaller buildings, so closely jammed together that it is almost impossible to see the narrow streets that twist between them'. Also, '. . . parks and open green spaces (so obvious as one flies above, say, London or Paris) are few and far between.'

Not visible but equally important to Tokyo 'style' is the lack of zoning – no slums and no ghettos, no good and bad sides of the tracks, no strictly industrial areas, no rigorously residential districts. The city, Seidensticker informs us, '. . . has always accommodated side by side the extremely well placed and the extremely poorly placed'. The bank and the pinball parlour, the beauty shop and the flophouse are juxtaposed.

All of this is because an overall plan, a civic ordering of the city, is missing. There is no imposed and consequently logical pattern. Tokyo seems the least designed of capitals, not so much contrived as naturally grown.

The West has only one city cultivated in this fashion, and that is Los Angeles. As critic Hunter Drohojowska has written: 'To know Los Angeles you must know Tokyo as well. Tokyo and Los Angeles are mirror cities, both wholly artificial, heavily reliant on surface appearances and essentially comfortable with life not as it was, but as it is.'

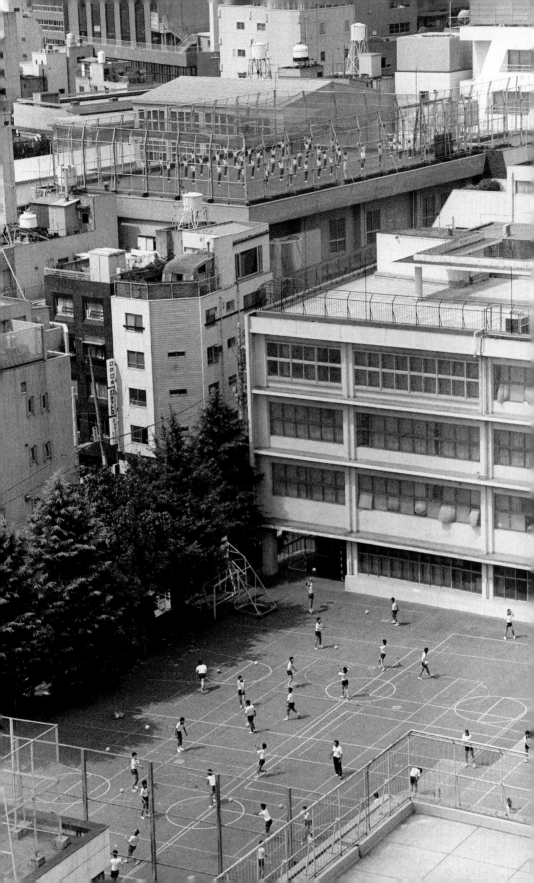

The model for the more ordinary modern Western city might have been something like a governmental report. The shape was the intent, with orderly statements leading to understood assumptions. There is little ambiguity, not much is left to chance, and the assertion is logical and conscious: a city has been built.

Such modern cities are, precisely, constructed. Paris under Napoleon III was officially remade into something more orderly than it had been. Before Baron Haussmann began his work in 1859, there were only a few straight boulevards – St-Denis, St-Martin, the rue de Rivoli. Napoleon's government, fearing popular insurrection, had the city planner build new avenues too wide to be barricaded, thus breaking up the poorer Parisians into neighbourhoods isolated from one another, thus constructing long avenues for the rapid bringing in of troops who could then take advantage of unbroken lines of fire. With Versailles as his model, Haussmann turned a monumental palace into a monumental city – just what the government wanted.

His real aim was the securing of the city against civil war. But his expressed urbanistic ideal was one of views in perspective down vistas. He, in a maneuvre described by Walter Benjamin, 'ennobled technical exigencies with artistic aims'.

Tokyo never took this step. One of the reasons might have been that there was never a civil war to loosen the web of property rights – something even the destruction of the Second World War failed to do. Yet at the same time, and unlike the original Paris, it was from the first a city of political intent. Indeed, it once actually had a plan, and this indicated its civic intentions.

Just as the Arab city is designed as an oasis and the medieval European city as a fortified market, there are cities created by fiat. Tokyo – like Washington or Beijing – was a city born of a decree. 'Here a city shall be built,' it was proclaimed, and so it was.

The centre of the capital still proclaims its origins. There sits the Imperial Palace, ubiquitous, directly in the centre, built on the site of Edo Castle. This is what the visitor sees as old Japan; this is what the resident must go around on the way home. It is the hub of the city, its core.

From the air, the palace grounds look like the Acropolis, the streets of Tokyo ebbing away from this centre as do the streets of Athens. It is like looking into a volcano; it is like looking down at the cross-section of an ancient tree-trunk.

There in Edo/Tokyo sits power, it would appear, surrounded by its inner moats, its outer ones having long since been swallowed by the city it sired. It is a real citadel, less imposing perhaps than that of Cairo, but apparently just as indestructible.

Grey stone walls, which in Greece would be called cyclopean, a few turrets, one of which is said to contain elements of the original castle, groves of pine and a recent swan in the ancient moat – all of this in the midst of grey Tokyo creates a metaphor.

Not at first, however. Edo Castle was not begun until 1603. Before that, the site was a small rise near a fishing village on the shores of a shallow bay. There, the waters lapping where the moat now stands, a daimyo named Ota Dokan, a retainer of one of the Ashikaga shoguns, built a modest residence. From its eminence, he could look down at the mouth of the Sumida River and, in the other direction, across the plains of Musashi.

Finished in 1458, this residence was apparently unpretentious as daimyo residences went. When Ota went to Kyoto to visit the Emperor in 1464, he wrote a poem that described the place:

> This house of mine
> Is in a grove of pine
> Along a blue sea,
> And from its simple eaves
> One sees high Fuji.

He was himself apparently just as unpretentious. A modern statue showing him life-size in a country-style sedge hat used to stand in front of the City Hall when it was located more or less in front of the Imperial Plaza. While the City Hall was being torn down a decade ago, Ota was exiled behind the Central Post Office. Now that the new City Hall stands in shining splendour in Shinjuku, he, still unpretentious, stands in the shadow of one of its towers.

Something more or less like this happened to Ota in real life as well. His castle was the strongest on the Kanto plain, and that plain was the site of several of Japan's richest provinces. But when the warlord Toyotomi Hideyoshi captured it, his palace was destroyed. The land – as always in Japan – was deemed more attractive than anything on it. His modest citadel became a prime building site.

Its fate was decided at Odawara, along the sea to the south, where Hideyoshi and fellow warlord Tokugawa Ieyasu discussed it in 1590. The former is supposed to have said that when the war was all over, he would give the latter the eight provinces of Kanto. Ieyasu, pleased, is said to have said: 'Good, let us piss on it.' This they did, side by side, on the battlements of the fallen Odawara Castle.

Thus was Edo born. Thus, too, the origin of a folk custom. Public urination is still common, and until recently men thus engaged side by side could be heard saying 'We are the pissers of Kanto' – a legacy from an earlier time.

Hideyoshi's motivation in offering such valuable land was that he wanted a free hand in Kyoto and knew what a dangerous rival Ieyasu might be. If Macbeth had been Japanese, he would not have murdered Banquo, but would have given him a small provincial castle far, far away. In the event, however, perhaps Macbeth's methods were better.

By 1600, Ieyasu had achieved military hegemony. By the following year, he had been named shogun and his government (the *bakufu*) had been established. He had already consoidated himself in Edo and had begun building his castle. The landfills at Hibiya Inlet were aleady completed and the moat well underway.

As shogun, Ieyasu could order all provincial daimyo to contribute men and materials. Some of the cyclopean stones were so enormous that a boat could only carry two and required 200 men to move them. Lumber was levied and the great castle itself was built: pure white stucco made from lime, grey clay tiles, with two enormous golden dolphins at the summit.

Such building required more and more space. The hills were levelled, the bay was pushed back, land was filled in. The castle grew and grew. It covered all of Ota's original site, all of the village of Edo, and kept on growing. Indeed, no matter how large it got – and by 1605 it was enormous, the largest castle in the world – there was never enough room.

There was the shogun and his entire cabinet; there were the daimyo, the provincial lords, and their retinues. This included not only their samurai but also all of their attendants. In addition, there were the craftsmen and servants who attended them and all of the merchants and peasants who provided for them. The castle was thus the architectural personification of an ideal feudalism, and Ieyasu himself was the apex of this pyramid of loyalties, a structure that lasted through all fifteen generations of the Tokugawa dynasty. But it did make something of a crowd.

By 1635, the shogunate had established the system of *sankin kotai,* which meant that daimyo should return to their home provinces, usually every other year. Ieyasu's plan was, however, not to relieve the crush in the castle, but to strengthen his centralized rule and thus weaken the role of the provincial daimyo.

Like Louis XIV at Versailles, he balanced his power by ensuring that those serving him spent all their money keeping two houses and travelling back and forth between them with full retinues. He even went one better than Louis. While making these long, expensive trips mandatory, he also insisted that wives and children (and an entire serving staff) be left behind in Edo as unacknowledged hostages.

The castle was filled to bursting: dozens of daimyo, hundreds of samurai, thousands of servants and other attendents, and no place to live but – eventually – outside the walls. By this time, the castle was no longer a fort. Ieyasu had conquered, had engineered an era of peace, a *pax Tokugawa*. Another reason the castle was no longer a fort was that it could never have withstood a seige. It was almost completely dependent on the outside for water and food.

Nonetheless, although the Tokugawa period is now viewed as

monolithic, with Edo controlling everything in a despotic manner, this was not the case. As the novelist Shiba Ryotaru has written:

> The notion that we Japanese all share the same values is a gross oversimplification. Creative thinking and social activism are the products of a society which honors pluralistic values . . . Each of the almost three hundred feudal domains into which Japan was divided boasted an individuality and diversity all its own.

This is not to say that there was no cultural uniformity; it existed in things like manners, etiquette, dress, hairstyles. Samurai were rather alike no matter where they were, but merchants and farmers were not. In actuality, the Tokugawa family was simply the leading power in an alliance of daimyo lords. Shiba has said that Saga (in the middle of Japan) and Satsuma (in the south) were like 'different countries'.

Nonetheless, from 1603 to 1867, Edo, the crammed castle in the centre, was the functioning capital. The first foreigners all assumed that it was indeed the real one and that the shogun was the ruler. Knowing nothing of Kyoto and the actual emperor there, Queen Victoria sent Ieyasu messages addressing him as 'His Imperial and Royal Majesty'.

The city was indeed the home of power, a capital in all but name. The new castle – the core of Edo – remains the core of Tokyo; the Imperial Palace still sits in three square kilometres of forest in the middle of the metropolis.

Early Edo looked very much like a citadel-city, a fort surrounded by walls and moats – and early seventeenth-century architecture was monumental, an expression of power. For this reason, the castle could easily adapt itself to sacred purposes when the time came for the investure of the Emperor in Edo/Tokyo in the mid-nineteenth century.

Many earlier citadel-cities – Athens, Sparta, Rome – were built around shrines. The god dwelt in the centre. In Tokyo, too, since the Emperor was until recently a god, his dwelling is holy, a shrine – and a powerful one.

Only a few generations ago, Tokyo citizens stopped in their tracks to bow in the direction of this imperial shrine, the palace. In spatial terms, they are still bowing since this area has never been menaced by developers even though it contains what would be the most expensive property on earth. Nor will the resident ever be evicted. Even now, at the beginning of the 21st century, the imperial house is inviolate. It is under taboo, and discussion as to its utility is never heard.

Such centrality is a baroque attribute, and one of the qualities of the baroque in any culture is an architectural display of power. Certainly, a garrison helped to build Tokyo just as a garrison helped to build modern Paris. Shogun Ieyasu would have agreed with Naples's King Ferrante who in 1475 characterized narrow streets as a danger to the State. Like Baron Haussmann, he wanted to make the city safe for its government.

This meant controlling land. New lots were allocated in what is now Nihombashi, and a straight road was extended from the Ote Gate to what is now Otemachi. The moat was enlarged to include Tamaike, then a fairly large pond, the place name of which remains. The daimyo were encouraged to build their estates all around the palace. What is now Marunouchi used to be called *daimyo-cho* because of these blocks of grand residences. One of the most splendid was supported by pillars carved to imitate cherry blossoms in full bloom, a carpentry feat much mentioned at the time.

By 1608, the palace had been extended all the way to Kudan, where Yasukuni Shrine is now. When finally finished, the shogun's residence was sixteen kilometres in circumference, its walls were pierced by sixty-six gates, and there were nineteen towers – part of one of which is still standing. The roof of the residence was 60 metres from the ground, and the donjon-keep – destroyed in 1657 and never restored – was a marvel. Inside, everything was fortified – gates, moats, bridges, walls, gardens, ponds, even a stage for the Noh.

Everything inside was ceremonial as well. As at Versailles, ritual ruled. Etiquette was of such acute importance that minor infractions were severely punished. The complicated plot machinery of

The Loyal Forty-Seven Ronin (a famous play still performed frequently at the Kabuki) gets its impetus not from an attempted murder but from a failure to observe proper etiquette.

There were reasons for such extraordinary ceremony. The Tokugawa state was a military hegemony, the longest lived the world has ever known. And like most hegemonies, this one found that the best insurance was bureaucracy and the most effective instrument was ritual.

Life in this hive became hugely complicated. In this world of ritual and ceremony, of intrigue and counter-intrigue, the castle could nearly be burnt down (as it was on several occasions) and yet court life would continue unchanged. When the temperate ('Regard all extravagance as your enemy. . .') Ieyasu died of stomach cancer (caused, it is said, by an extreme frugality of diet), life went on just as he had designed it.

The centre of the new capital remained the castle itself. The general form of the surrounding city, observed an early visitor, W. E. Griffes, in 1876, 'is that of an egg with the point to the south, butt to the north. The yoke of this egg is the castle . . .' All roads led to it, though not in the straightforword manner of Washington, D.C. Rather, the roads surrounded the castle core, like the rings of a tree, and one may even now read the history of the place by examining these concentric circles.

Retainers moved down into these circular streets and were joined (the rings spreading) by the servitors and tradesmen who waited on them and on the castle. As the city grew so did the rings round the core. These became less and less circular as convenience stretched them to and fro, as they were crossed by more expedient paths, shortcuts curtailing the curving avenues. Slowly, the purely military pattern turned civilian and then into that tangled array typical of the needs of free trade and capitalism. It was as though L'Enfant's Washington had, once past the White House, reverted to the paths and lanes of rural Virginia.

The core and a few of the ring roads exist even now, but elsewhere a different pattern of growth has prevailed. This pragmatic shape means that little thought is given to overall form, to political logic or to civic beautification. This is something that earlier travellers, looking for some kind of visible civic intention, found wanting.

In 1886, John La Farge wrote of 'this big dreary city of innumerable little houses'; six years earlier, Isabella Bird had written of Tokyo that '. . . as a city it lacks concentration.' It was, she found, 'a city of magnificent distances without magnificence'.

There were, and are, few vistas. The city simply pushed itself west to the plains or east to reclaimed land in the bay. The need for short-term advantage rather than long-range planning resulted in a city haphazard and natural – if that means 'allowed to grow as it will undisciplined by a municipal plan'.

Today, few patterns of original Edo are visible. One – besides the castle core and the ring-like roads – that still exists is the bifurcation of the city, perhaps not part of the original intention but an aspect that has done much to create the city's character.

This bifurcation occurred as the shogun and his officials decided to grant most of the more salubrious and hilly portions of the new city to the military aristocracy and the newly filled-in delta flatlands of the bay and river to the merchants and craftsmen who purveyed and laboured. These latter lands became the Shitamachi. The name means 'towns below' and refers to those areas beneath the castle but still within the city limits. Edward Seidensticker has felicitously translated the term as 'Low City' – the hills became the Yamanote, the 'High City'. He has also estimated that the Low City, which gave Edo so much of its character, only occupied about one-fifth of the city.

It now occupies even less, the High City has grown so much. Yet the traditional Low City perseveres, even now remaining different in feeling from the Westernized Yamanote. Now comprised (according to the Shitamachi Museum) of Kanda, Nihombashi, Kyobashi, Shitaya (Ueno), Asakusa, Honjo and Fukagawa, it still retains what little is left of the feel of old Edo – distinctly plebian, also fun-loving, less inhibited than those remains of areas where the military aristocracy, the shogunate, observed its rules of decorum. Paul Waley has said that even in the Meiji period, long after Westernization, people going to the Low City still spoke of 'going to

23

Edo'. The area is, in this sense, something like a medina or a souk, a place where it all began, a place of commerce, of mingling.

So, just when the medieval city was being destroyed in Europe in favour of municipalities more visibly planned, Tokyo was evolving into something we would call medieval. After the fall of the Shogunate in 1867, growth was governed by necessity rather than decree. Though the succeeding government representing the Emperor Meiji looked to the West and attempted some modest city planning, the only laws truly followed were those of pragmatic need. Even now, as one leaves the castle one plunges into the warren.

There are, to be sure, some straight streets, square blocks, properly named and numbered. These are the results of sporadic municipal concern. The Ginza, the Marunouchi business district, the Seijo and Denenchofu residental districts – these evidence a brief civic ambition. Otherwise, little planning is visible.

Some modern cities elsewhere are segregated on the basis of difference – ethnic, religious, social. But this kind of manufacturing of neighbourhoods is also not seen frequently in Japanese cities. Degrees of difference which are indicated geographically all have to do with commodities. One still buys cloth at Suda-cho, one banks at Otemachi, old books are found in Kanda, fish at the Tsukiji fish market. All of this one sees elsewhere in the city as well, but it is in these districts that the actual remains of the mercantile guilds are still found.

For rational, planned, logical castle-town Edo to turn so quickly into unplanned, illogical Tokyo indicates that modernization is in large part a dismantling, a destruction rather than a construction. The logical construction which Tokugawa Ieyasu envisioned for his new capital was in this sense modernized into the random, seemingly aimless, overcrowded mercantile metropolis that has resulted in Tokyo.

Those who refer to the winding streets of . . . a town as mere tracings of the cowpath do not realize that the cow's habit of following contours usually produces a more economical and sensible layout . . . than any inflexible system of straight streets.

24

Lewis Mumford's observation indicates the structure which Tokyo, once away from the castle, was evolving, not only in what had been swamp, the Low City, but in the High City as well. Edward Seidensticker has remarked that a map of this area 'puts one in mind of a vast, ancient country village, with the streets following animal tracks and the boundaries of fields . . .'

The contours (cow paths crossing) were largely mercantile, and small nodes of commerce grew around the silk warehouses, the vegetable market, the charcoal sellers' district. These were like connected villages, the web of the residential capital growing among them. Comparable to the European medieval city, the sixteenth-century Japanese capital was eventually a congeries of little towns, each with some degree of self-sufficiency, each formed so naturally from common needs that the whole was enriched.

The small communities of Edo, formed by mercantile interests, evolved their own necessary parts: the town hall, the public bath, the goods store, the market, the pleasure district. Though such self-sufficient groupings have largely vanished in the centralized Western city, they remain visible in the Japanese one. Tokyo is filled with (or composed of) such small, self-contained communities.

Almost no foreign observer even now fails to discover in Tokyo a city of villages. Henry D. Smith II has collected a number; Isabella Bird called Tokyo an 'aggregate of one hundred twenty-five villages', though how she discovered this precise number is not known; in 1930, Peter Quennell found a 'huge extension of a single neighborhood'; in 1976, David Riesman discovered a 'metropolis superimposed on a series of small villages'.

Indeed, foreigners became so knowledgeable that the novelist Junichiro Tanizaki (quoted by Seidensticker) could complain that '. . . foreigners and Japanese alike denounced our capital city as "not a city but a village, or a collection of villages."' One of the reasons this kind of city structure is so often mentioned is that it is so plainly evident.

Such an urban pattern was perhaps once worldwide, but it is now no longer found in Western cities, where units are welded together to create residential areas, business areas and so on. In Japan, only modernized in the last century, these units remain independent; hence the feeling of proceeding through village after village, each with its own main street: a bank, a supermarket, a flower shop, a pinball parlour, all without street names or numbers because villagers don't need them.

Each complex is a small town, and their numbers make up this enormous capital. Like cells in a body, each contains identical elements, and the resulting pattern is an organic one. No town planner has yet altered this natural order.

It is possible to see in this something like a national characteristic. One can find in the cell-like structure of Tokyo something of the cell-like structure of the country and of the life of its inhabitants. As Kurt Singer has said, let the Westerner sincerely try to live by Japanese customs 'and he will instantly feel what a cell endowed with rudiments of human sensibility must be supposed to feel in a well-coordinated body'.

Just as the Japanese themselves can – and perhaps should – be seen as a tribe, or a collection of tribes, so their cities may be seen as integrated ensembles of small communities. This is as true of such small collections as Sapporo and Kagoshima as it is of that megapolis which now extends from Tokyo-Yokohama to Osaka-Kyoto.

The dwellers themselves are of several minds about their cities. Teshigahara Hiroshi has said that all Japanese cities 'are in a true state of disorder. There is not one in Japan which is constructed on any regular plan. There is no aesthetic harmony, there are no standards at all'. Abe Kobo wrote that Tokyo itself is 'a limitless number of villages. These villages and their people all appear identical. So no matter how far you walk you seem to remain where you started, going nowhere at all. And wherever you are in Tokyo you lose your way'. Tanizaki had the mad old man in one of his novels refer to 'that overturned rubbish heap of a Tokyo'. And that finest of Tokyo chroniclers, Nagai Kafu, wrote that '. . . it would seem that we Japanese are wholly lacking in the ability to build a city.'

Tokyo had many opportunities to build a city. Tanizaki was pleased with the 1923 earthquake and thought it would afford

26

the opportunity to construct a metropolis he could admire. Nothing of the sort occurred. When the city was destroyed again, this time in the spring of 1945 by American B-29's, another occasion occurred. I remember well what Tokyo was like after its destruction in the Second World War. Here are some pages from my journal:

February 28, 1947, Winter – cold, crisp, clear – and Fuji stands sharp on the horizon, growing purple, then indigo in the fading light. I stand at the main crossing on the Ginza, nothing between me and the mountain. It is clear because there is no smoke, few factories, no fumes because the few cars are charcoal-burning. Fuji looks much as it must have for Hokusai and Hiroshige.

I stand and watch the mountain fade. From this crossing it had not been seen since Edo times; but now all the buildings in between are cinders. Between me and Fuji is a burned waste-land, a vast and blackened plain where a city had once stood.

At this crossing there are only two large buildings standing. The Ginza branch of the Mitsukoshi Department Store, gutted, hit by a fire-bomb, even the window frames twisted by the heat. Across the street is the other, the white stone Hattori Building with its clock tower: much as it had been with its cornices and pediments.

There is not much else left: the ruins of the burned-out Kabuki-za, the round, red, drum-like Nichigeki, undamaged. At Yurakucho, on the edge of the Ginza, are a few office buildings and the Tokyo Takarazuka Theatre, now renamed the Ernie Pyle, and the Hibiya and Yurakuza motion-picture theatres.

Otherwise block after block of rubble, stretching to the horizon. Wooden buildings did not survive the fire storms of the American bombers. Those that stood were made of stone or brick. Yet, already, among these there is the yellow sheen of new wood. People are returning to the city.

I see them shuffling along the pavements, all those now returning. One somehow expects festivity – there were so many people shambling along or lounging about. But there are no laughter and little conversation. And it is dark, this Ginza which had once been a fountain of light. Now it is lit only by the passing headlights of Occupation jeeps and trucks, and the acetylene torches in the night stalls.

Here everything is being sold – the products of a vanished civilization. There were wartime medals and egret feather tiaras and top hats and beaded handbags. There were bridles and bits and damascene cufflinks. There were ancient brocades and pieces of calligraphy, battered woodblock prints and old framed photographs. Everything is for sale – or for barter.

Stopping, looking, handling, passing, were the people. Uniforms are still everywhere – black student uniforms, army uniforms, young men wearing their forage caps, or their army boots, or their winter-issue overcoats; others were in padded kimono, draped with scarves; women still in kimono or those *mompe* trousers used for farm work which in the cities had served as wartime dress. And many wear face-masks because of winter colds. Also, everyone was out of fashion: in peacetime they are still dressed for war.

How quiet the crowd is. The only sounds are the scufflings of boots, shoes, wooden sandals. These and the noises of the merchandise being picked up, turned over, put down. The merchants make no attempt to sell. They sit and look, smoking a pinch of tobacco in long-stemmed brass pipes, staring at the black throng passing in the darkness of an early evening.

I look at faces: an old woman illuminated by a passing truck, the white profile of a young student in the acetylene glare, a mother, the blank round faces of her two children. Well over a year had passed since the unthinkable occurred and the unendurable endured. I was regarding a populace still in shock. There was an uncomprehending look in the eyes. It was a look one sometimes still sees in the eyes of children or the very ill.

And in the eyes of convalescents as well. Shacks are being built, any which way, new streets are formed, a hut here, a shack there. Yet Tokyo is a city of the dead. So many were killed, so many were burned or boiled in the fire-bomb raids. The survivors remembered.

But at the same time the dead are being forgotten, as they must be if we are to go on living. Everyday, the crowd is larger, the eyes get brighter, Tokyo grows.

I sometimes pause on that corner now, look at all the tall buildings, all that glass and marble and steel, and remember what it was like before – the soft shuffle of the crowd, the smell of charcoal burning. Then the sky would darken and the stars appear – bright, near. The horizon stayed white in the winter light after the sun had vanished and Fuji turned a solid black.

Affluent Tokyo – and it remains a rich city despite its various recessions and its homeless – is an example of a modern industrial capital. It exemplifies Aristotle's remark, in *The Politics*, that '. . . a city is composed of different kinds of men; similar people cannot bring a city into existence.'

Indeed, one can learn much about the people of Tokyo by looking at their city. They are industrious, wasteful, impatient, gregarious, lavish, enthusiastic, given to following the latest fads and always lamenting the past. Their common contradictions, their heights of aspiration and their lows of comprehension prove Rousseau's dictum that '. . . houses make a town, but citizens make a city.'

The resulting vitality is such that if one loves Tokyo, one loves it for its people. Indeed, one might say of the Japanese capital (as Dr Johnson said of London): 'When a man is tired of it, he is tired of life.'

This vitality is largely economic. It is based, however, not so much on wealth as on the growth of wealth. All the mechanics of Japanese society are sustained in this way. The continual growth of wealth is both the support and the means of this society. This in turn is based upon raw materials that can be made into goods, or into more wealth. Here, land is the main source of sustained and growing wealth, but the amount of land is limited just as wealth is limited. Indeed, everything is finite. Fujii Nobuo, the economist whom I have been paraphrasing here, ends his argument by observing that '. . . this affluent society is built upon a flaw.'

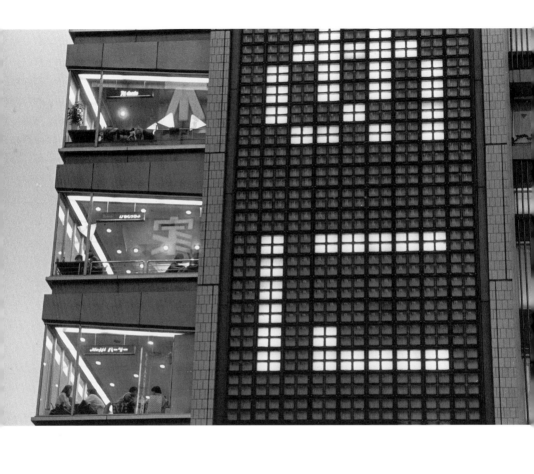

Although this is now becoming evident, Tokyo remains a mercantile capital – one where the concentration of corporate headquarters in the centre of the city has so inflated land prices that the residents have been squeezed out. The fact that people are still pouring into Tokyo, anxious to live here, has been seen (again by Fujii) not so much as the result of personal needs as the consequence of the businessman's will to locate offices in the central wards of the city in proximity to the central government's offices, whose policies can have a definite effect on all businesses.

Waley has noted that since 1950, the population of the place has doubled, as has what planners call the doughnut phenomenon: the daytime population of the inner wards of the city (Chiyoda, Chuo, Minato) is six times higher than the population at night.

Thus this overcrowded city with its substandard ('rabbit-hutch') housing, its inconveniences, its lack of breathing spaces, its sometimes near-chaos, does say something about its inhabitants. Perhaps it tells us that Tokyo has never been seen by those who live in it as the monster that New York or London sometimes appears to be – a place to be avoided, not to be inhabited, merely to be visited for work.

Londoners actually want to live in the suburbs where they have a bit of space, a spot of green. New Yorkers also have their reasons for preferring Rye and Westhampton. Tokyoites, however, want to live in Tokyo, always have, always will. For them the suburbs (where the majority of the working force live) and the long commute exist only because they cannot afford to live in crowded, expensive Tokyo.

Not for them the apocalyptic view of the city, as Friedrich Engels so expressively described it: 'A town such as London, where a man might wander for hours together without reaching the beginning of the end, without meeting the slightest hint which could lead to the inference that there is open country within reach, is a strange thing.'

Not at all. The Japanese are the new nomads. Workers travel up to two or three hours a day between sleeping place and working place. This does not create the nomadic mentality, however, where you stay until you use everything up and then move on. The Japanese practise a kind of oscillation – one half fills up again while you are occupying the other. This does entail a certain kind of rootlessness. One does not become attached to the bedroom community merely because one goes to bed in it. Besides, there are only suburbs out there.

The closer to the middle of the city the better. Thus the prices of property. Mark Girouard has observed that an aerial view of Manhattan is 'a three-dimensional diagram of property values and rent levels', expensive skyscrapers in the middle spreading out to the cheaper reaches of the Bronx and Brooklyn. Tokyo is the same, except that it all tends to be expensive near any node of transportation, no matter how far out.

There is really nowhere to get a proper view of Tokyo. In Paris, one climbs up to the Sacre-Coeur; there, seen from the top of Montmartre, is the whole city – visible, discrete, understandable. In Rome, there are seven hills to choose among, each with a view of the Eternal City. Similar city views abound in Budapest, San Francisco, Edinburgh.

There is, to be sure, Tokyo Tower, and the tops of assorted Shinjuku skyscrapers as well, but from these heights there is no unified panorama. Nor could there be – not only is Tokyo too large and sprawling, it is also too undifferentiated. One cannot look down upon Tokyo as upon a living map as one can in Kobe and Hakodate. Nor can one assume an order one cannot see, as in Kyoto. It is difficult to comprehend cities you cannot see all of from somewhere.

Nor is it easy to get proper views of any of Tokyo's main sections. The main streets are not about providing vistas. The grand sight of an entire avenue – 'one of the most glorious sights for state and magnificence that any city can show a traveller', as John Evelyn discovered in 1644 when he saw Rome's Via Pia – is not for the Japanese.

It is not that magnificence is not for the Japanese, but that public magnificence is not. The truly magnificent is, in Tokyo as in Edo, always found in private. Historically, the reason for a lack of public

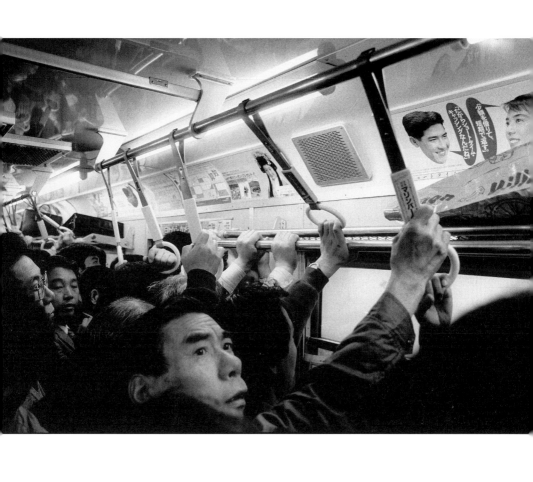

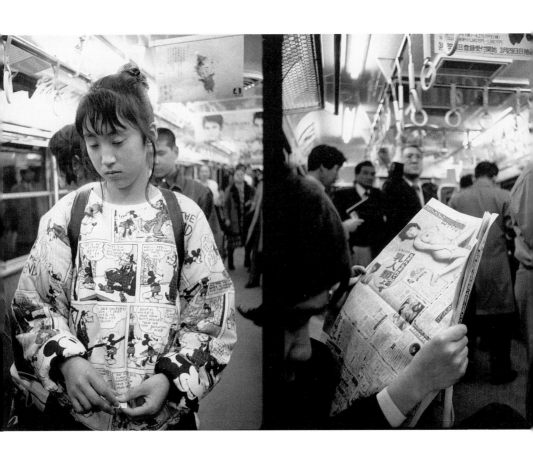

display was that it was not necessary to impress a populace already impressed. Edo had no political reason for a vista.

In the same way, there was never any need to beautify Tokyo. In the ordinary Western capital, there seems to be an agreed-upon notion that beauty should at least be attempted, that being beautiful is one of the aims of the architecture. In Tokyo, beauty was never a public concern, not in the sense that it is in, say, Paris. Being modern and being ostentatious were obviously architectural concerns from the Meiji period on, but not being beautiful. In fact, though Edo had a certain plain charm due to the coherence of building materials, Tokyo is unusually ugly.

The modern city, from the Meiji period through the succeeding Taisho and on to the earthquake of 1923, was 'a sham hallway, a grand façade with nothing behind it, a device for deceiving the foolish'. There is no reason to regret its having been reduced to ashes:

> The Japanese people had already lost their dwelling; their national treasure-house was by way of becoming nothing. Concerned only about outward decorations, a country that has been unable to make long-range plans should expect to meet such a fate . . .

– this being a summation by Nagai Kafu as quoted by Edward Seidensticker in that finest of Tokyo books, *Kafu the Scribbler*.

When the country initially was opened to the West (to the extent that it was) after the middle of the nineteenth century, a few European esplanades were attempted. The gingko-lined boulevard leading into Meiji Park, that grand avenue leading to the Diet Building – these are late promenades, but they are too short to be really grand. And they continue to share something with the sham hallway of which Kafu complained.

Edo too had few concourses affording splendid vistas. Not that the city did not have its views. These were celebrated in poem and picture: Mt Fuji seen from Nihon Bridge, the flowering cherries of Ueno seen from the Kaneiji Kiyomizu-do. Such sights, however, remained unconnected with vistas.

Nothing was made, for example, of the most promising material.

35

Aoyama-dori is a wide, straight avenue, stretching from Akasaka to Shibuya. From a mid-point on a clear day, one may see Fuji framed at the apex of the avenue, a splendid sight at the end of an impressive vista. In any other city, much would be made of this. Not in Tokyo, however. A vista is a municipal construction, and this is of little interest to the people going about making their livings and living their lives.

In any event, the streets are usually too narrow and too crooked to make satisfactory vistas. The Ginza at its widest, for example, is less than 30 metres, as compared with the Champs-Elysées, which is 70. The Ginza sidewalks are just over six metres wide, vast for Japan but narrow compared to those of the Parisian boulevard, nearly twelve metres.

Otherwise, the streets of Tokyo are often too narrow to contain proper sidewalks. The walker feels much as Walter Benjamin did in Moscow when he noted that '. . . nowhere else except in Naples, do you find sidewalks this narrow.'

As there is no vista, there is likewise no promenade. Just as there is no public display of stately buildings, so there is no place set aside for stately walking about. Nothing like Fifth Avenue once was, nothing like the middle way of the Tuileries in nineteenth-century Paris or the Boulevard St-Antoine in the eighteenth.

There is the Ginza, but this avenue was never intended as a civil promenade; it was intended as a commercial promenade. In contemporary Tokyo, the only promenades are those more or less constructed by the inhabitants: the Sunday-afternoon gatherings at Yoyogi Park near Harajuku, the Friday-evening routs at Roppongi crossing.

If Edo had no promenades, it was because one was meant to see and be seen only in private – at the castle and at the better residences. Walking about for the entire populace to gape at would have been considered ill bred. The Emperor Meiji attempted to take strolls outside his new Tokyo palace, but was soon stopped because such exposure was unheard of. Anonymity in the street was the rule. Women of means travelled by closed palanquin, and high-ranking men went partially disguised if they were walking – particularly if strolling around Edo's single large promenade, the Yoshiwara prostitutes' quarter.

Tokyo streets do not speak in the measured accents of Europe's capitals and such European-inspired cities as Washington, D.C. Bernard Rudofsky observed that a street is 'no better than the company of houses it keeps', that '. . . skyscrapers and empty lots do not a city make,' and that '. . . a perfect street is harmonious space.' True, but in Tokyo skyscrapers and empty lots do make a city, and in place of harmonious space it is possible to have congenial variety and vitality.

If the European street can be something like a stage, the Japanese street is like a market. This is very Asian of it. Shops line the street, open up, spill out. Clothes on racks and sides of beef alike are shoved onto sidewalks. The fish shop's scaly glitter is right there, still gasping. Baby televisions, miniature computers piled high blink eye to eye. Not here, not yet, the closed transactions of the supermarket; instead, the raw profusion of consumption itself exists right out on the street.

And even along the more sedate avenues, including the Ginza itself where the goods are kept indoors, the promiscuous display continues. Hoardings bellow, flags and banners yell, neon points and *kanji* grabs. Signs are everywhere, all of them shouting – a semiotic babble, signifiers galore. The foreign walker must feel much as G. K. Chesterton said he felt upon first seeing Broadway: 'What a glorious garden of wonder this would be to anyone who was lucky enough to be unable to read.'

This profusion, this advertisement, this babble is very Asian of the Japanese street. And we would recognize it if the 'units' were mangoes or rice cakes. But here they are calculators and microwave ovens, instant cameras and word processors.

Yet it is still the street we read about in the novels of Saikaku and see in the prints of Hokusai. In old Edo, the main street was called a *noren-gai*. The better shops advertised themselves with their *noren*, entry-curtains marked with the shop crest. The concept remains.

The *noren* may be façade-high neon, the metres-long laser

beam, but the *gai* is still marked as a place of display. From Ginza's shop-window showcases to the piles of silicon chips out on the Akihabara (Electric City) sidewalk like exotic nuts, the display continues.

The Japanese street, whatever it lacks in municipal presence, remains an ideal to which all commercial venues must aspire. It is the ultimate in unrestrained display. Other streets in other countries may strive for this riot, but they are handicapped by zoning laws, by citizens' associations and the like. Not so Tokyo, or not to the same extent. The Japanese street is very public.

The reason is that the Japanese home is very private. In Edo, all the better houses had fences, and in Tokyo many still do. Though suburbia must content itself with token hedges and ornamental walls, privacy is still respected. House and garden (if there is one) are private property in the most closed and restricted sense. In a city as crowded as Tokyo (or Edo), privacy is a luxury almost as expensive as space. What is acquired at great cost is jealously guarded.

This might be regarded as a national characteristic. Kurt Singer found it so. Certainly, he wrote, '. . . no people could be less entitled to complain of being misunderstood, unknown, or neglected than the Japanese, whose first and last urge is to lead a life unseen by others.' Japanese writings, he observed, suggest rather than express; traditional singing demands the repression of the voice; and '. . . in every gesture of daily life, in the style of conversation, in the proper form of giving a present, the rule, it seems, is how to wrap up things, ideas, and feelings.' Wherever the Japanese people go, '. . . they make a network of walls and fences behind which to retire: unwritten rules, ceremonies, and taboos.'

If what is thus enclosed is private, then what is not is public. So it is in Western cities as well. The difference is one of degree. In Japan, private space is seen as so sacrosanct that public space is regarded as profane. Something which belongs to everyone belongs to no-one.

As a consequence, there are few effective zoning laws, small civic endeavours, little city planning. While houses are subject to strict scrutiny, the surrounding streets are not. These are thus allowed

38

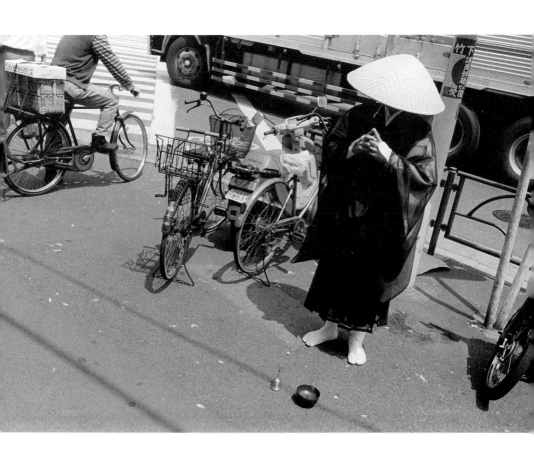

an organic life of their own. They proliferate, and street life takes on unrestricted, natural forms.

In this sense, much of Tokyo is a grand warren, a twisted tangle of alleys and lanes. Though there are some grid-patterned sections where civic endeavour has attempted to create order, this enormous city is a comfortable rat's nest. Streets have grown as old Edo dictated and as convenience now directs. Opportunities to remake the city have been resisted – not only after the various Edo disasters but also after the 1923 earthquake and the 1945 fire-bombing.

One reason, of course, is that the warren is preferred. It was seen (or felt) to be a proper human environment. The Japanese, like the English, prefer the cozy, and consequently the streets of new Tokyo are as crooked and twisting as those of old London. There is a corresponding sense of group: our cozy warrens are just for us, not for those of you outside.

In their interiors, many Japanese still insist upon a rigid distinction (almost English in its inflexibility) between public and private. Take, for example, the fact that one is required almost everywhere to leave one's shoes at the door. Explanations abound. It is more hygienic and we are a clean people; it shows respect and we are a respectful people; such a place is, as it were, sacred and we are a religious people. Another reason has been offered by Shuji Takashina: 'Rather than say that the Japanese use the floor for a bed . . . it might be more accurate to say that they use [the] bed for a home.'

Whatever the proffered reason, however (all of them are true), one fact remains. Taking off your shoes indelibly marks the end of the public and the beginning of the private. This is an important distinction. George Bernard Shaw is remembered, in that he is recalled at all in Japan, for the certainly apocryphal story that during a trip here in the 1930s he refused to shed his footwear and strode in brogues across the virgin mats.

Which concern is what one might expect from a people who make so much of what is private (ours) and so little of what is public (theirs). For such folk, the neighbourhood is of primary importance.

40

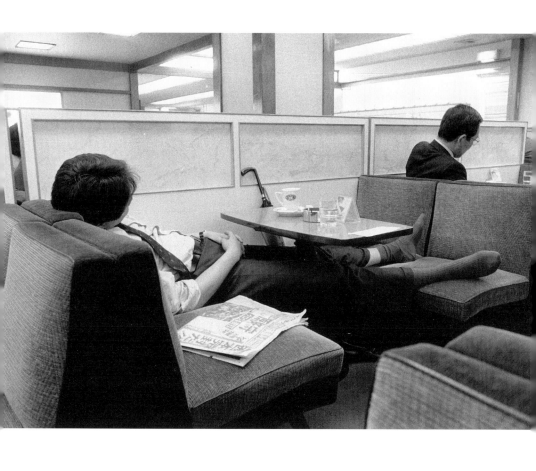

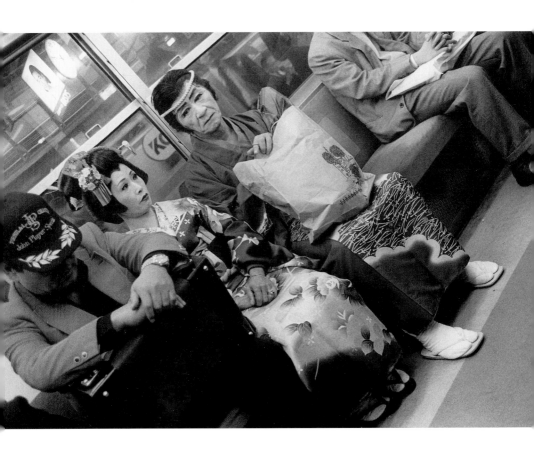

When a section is torn down (since the value of Tokyo land is sometimes higher than the native Tokyo feeling for the burrow is strong), it is interesting that though the new big building may be four-square and right-angled (since such buildings are now more cheaply constructed), parts of the original warren are duplicated (dry cleaner, beauty parlour, chemist) in the basement.

One of the results of public areas belonging to no-one is that they belong to everyone and can be so used. This means that owners or leasers of private land in public places may be as idiosyncratic as they please. Those foreign visitors who have been told that there is such a thing as monolithic Japan, that all the people there look, act, feel and are alike, are always surprised by the extraordinary variety of urban architecture. Given what they may have heard of the Japanese character, they come expecting conformity and are presented with the wildest diversity. A glass-and-concrete box (a cosmetics outlet) is next to a traditional tile-roofed restaurant (*sukiyaki* and *shabu-shabu*), which is next to a hi-tech open-girder construction (a boutique), which is next to a pastel-plastered French provincial farmhouse (designer clothes and a tea-room). This can seem threatening, as in one of Borges's labyrinths where the impression is

> that of the interminable, that of the atrocious, that of the completely senseless . . . it abounded in dead-end corridors, high unattainable windows, portentious doors which led to a cell or pit, incredible inverted stairways whose steps and balustrades hung downwards. Other stairways, clinging airily to the side of a monumental wall, would die without leading anywhere . . .

Kafu noticed this at the beginning of the century, when he wrote that '. . . there have been trains and streetcars and factories, but that art of the people known as architecture has been quite destroyed.' In its place was the modern building. Built to attract attention, it had (and has) the same function as the signs and banners that also sometimes decorate it. To stand out is to sell something more effectively. As for conformity, well, there is plenty of that, but not in anything so superficial as architecture.

43

Actually, despite the architectural results, construction methods remain conservative. The boldest flights are grounded in traditional methods. The most traditional of these, one which stretches back into history and which permeates almost all Japanese endeavour, is that which we recognize as modular construction.

'If the domestic house is the microcosm of the city, so the city is the home writ large,' said Donald Olsen, and in the deployment of space and the construction of what is conceived as a whole, Japan is no different from anywhere else. The Japanese house is much like the Japanese city, also composed of modules.

In the traditional dwelling, the components are always of the same nature, the same size, module-like. The tatami mats, the *fusuma* doors, the shoji windows, the *amado* shutters are of invariable proportion, built to fit every home. And this module-mindedness continues even today when new apartments contain neither tatami nor *amado*. The rooms are now built-up ferro-concrete or pre-cast plastic lowered into place, each one identical – the carpenters now tighten bolts rather than saw and fit, but the modular principle remains the same.

The Japanese are, more than most, a module people. The language, the thought itself tends to modular forms: the cliché is respected, the ritual is observed; most of the arts – Japanese dance, the martial arts – are taught in the form of modules called *kata*. One wonders at the origin of this. Is it perhaps the pragmatic advantage of form? Invariable observations oil the machinery of human relations; modular construction lowers unit cost. What is now true of computer parts was once true of tatami sizes and remains true of seasonal compliments. And each unit is, within the confines of its genre, complete.

Complete but impermanent. The visitor, attention turned from spatial to temporal considerations, soon senses that, though now such permanent materials as stone, steel and marble are used, the city does not appear as though it has been built to last.

In the days of wood and roof tile, the nature of the materials implied a certain morality. But now, though the materials have

44

changed, fallibility still seems to be assumed. The habits of the old wood culture are maintained even though wood is now too expensive to use.

Back when Edo was wooden, fires were common. Every decade had its devastation, great swathes burned through the city. This rarely resulted in fire-breaks (though that straight, wide avenue, the Ginza, with its original fireproof brick buildings, resulted from the 1872 conflagration), but one consequence was to think of construction materials as expendable and to fold the idea of impermanence into architecture. Even now that concrete is a common material, the goal is not permanence.

The Federation of Housing Production Organizations conducted a survey and found, in the words of a 1998 *Japan Times* report, that '. . . private houses in Japan stand an average of twenty-six years before their owners knock them down and build anew.' Many owners 'would prefer it if they could live in the same house for fifty years', it was reported. The fact that they do not indicates that permanence is not a goal; two-and-a-half decades are still enough.

A relevant factor is that the land itself, so expensive, must be, as it were, renewed. Properties over a decade old rapidly lose their value. It is for this reason that there is little serious investment in better housing. Also, property taxes are low, and land used for crops is barely taxed at all. Thus owners tend to sit on their land. Somehow it has been decided that about one-eighth of enormous Tokyo is still being 'farmed'. This means that empty lots make money, and the savings can be used to finally build on them.

In another sense, the feeling of transience in Tokyo has an equally firm base. The city rests on more than nineteen different active faults, any one of which could set off major earthquakes at any time. The last major earthquake disaster in Tokyo occurred in 1923, when the city was partially destroyed and an estimated 142,000 inhabitants were killed. There are now over twelve million people in daytime Tokyo, and fatalities could be correspondingly high.

Even without such graphic disasters, there are many reminders that Tokyo is a fragile and transient metropolis. Heavy rains immediately flood the streets; heavy snows always produce chaos. '1,664

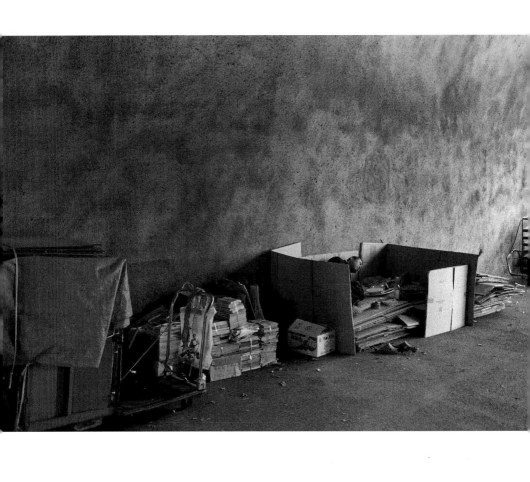

trains suspended, 410,000 passengers inconvenienced . . . 38 people require ambulence service, 1,200 households without power, more that 310 flights cancelled' – all of this because of a minor snow flurry which deposited sixteen centimetres on the city. Invariably, the headlines read 'Snow Wreaks Havoc Across Tokyo Again.' In part, the havoc is due to an ordinary lack of human concern – traffic jams, wearing high heels on the ice, etc. But in greater part, it is because Tokyo has very little infrastructure equipped to cope with the unexpected. Administrative offices work less well with each other than they do in other major cities in the world; there is less accountability in the Japanese system, and the buck, rather than stopping, circulates endlessly. People in Tokyo exclaim: 'If a snowstorm can do all this, just think what an earthquake could do!'

More than most cities, Tokyo thus lives with an apprehension of its own destruction. Perhaps some of the frenetic life of the city, the feeling of dancing on the edge of a volcano, is a result of this knowledge. Certainly, a part of the apathy, the lack of preparedness, is due to a general awareness of inevitability.

This air of the transient, so noticeable in the Japanese city, is enforced in that traditional Japanese architectural styles are rarely seen. New buildings are constructed in fashions so flamboyantly modern that one cannot but expect them to be superseded.

In new Tokyo, unlike old Edo, no unity of architectural style is attempted or achieved. Just as some Japanese are meticulous about family or office but neglect what we might call civic duties, buildings are complete within themselves, and no attempt is made to harmonize them with either their setting or those structures adjacent to them.

Hence the random appearance of the modern Japanese city – just one individual expression after another. The reason for the feeling of unreality experienced by Westerners is that their assumptions concerning urban grammar are not there to be read. After all, the buildings do not 'fit' the streets – rectangular edifices located on curved byways always result in singular effects.

On observing people on the street in Tokyo, a foreign fashion designer, quoted by Peter Popham, said that '. . . the clothes are

47

beautiful, but the people are not really *wearing* them yet.' There was something, he added, not quite modern about that.

Tokyo architecture is like this. There is something not quite modern about it. Also, not quite real. Consequently, Japanese cities often feel like the back lots of movie studios. The various sets, all of them quite large and seemingly permanent, are constructed, used and left standing. There seems to be no reason for their arrangement. They were built for reasons of economy and convenience, and there is no unifying style because the uses of each were different. Though they look sturdy, they were not made to last – and indeed they will not.

The Western municipality which Tokyo most resembles is the only 'city' the West erects in the knowledge that it will not last: the international exposition, where massive buildings are thrown up, avenues are constructed, and vast crowds are accommodated, but only for a season. The assumption is that all of this will shortly be pulled down. Building only for now, and only for show, architects are encouraged to be extreme. Tokyo is like an international exposition which has remained standing.

It can be melancholy in the same fashion. As Nagai Kafu noted (in Lane Dunlop's translation) in his 1931 novel, *During the Rains*, '. . . when a city aped the West to the degree that Tokyo did, the spectacle provoked in the observer is an astonishment, along with a certain sense of pathos.'

In Tokyo, the buildings are mostly modern Western, but their urban grid is not. The architectural style is visionary futuresque, but the urban structure remains medieval. The civic organization is thus, in Western terms, primitive. Extremely contemporary-looking structures are like nomads' tents, with the difference that the Japanese move not through space but through time.

It has been said that a great city is the best organ of memory that humanity has yet devised. But if, as Emerson observed, a city 'lives by remembering', then amnesiac Tokyo would be dead. A city can live in many ways other than by remembering.

And as for being primitive, there is no doubt that Japanese cities

48

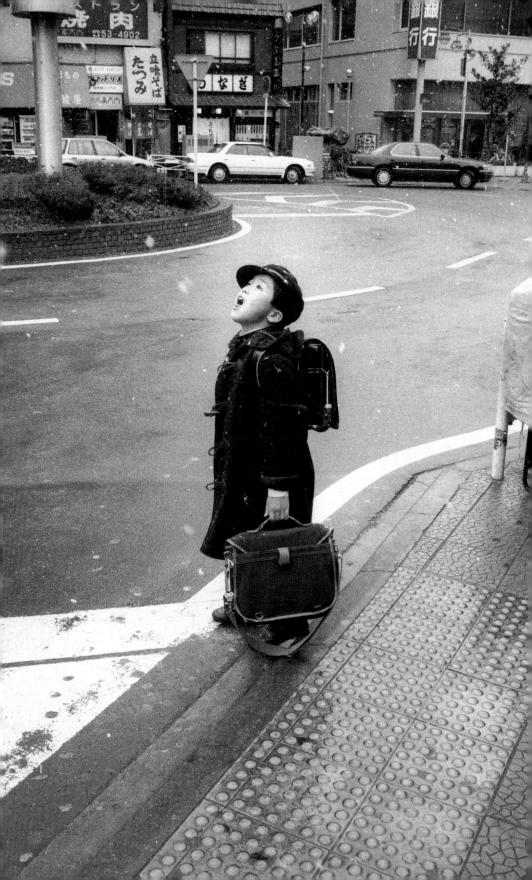

continue to exhibit a stage of urban development much earlier than than of the contemporary West. But this primitivism is not to be thought of in perjorative terms. It may be more simple, but it is also more natural. Certainly, once comprehended, the Japanese city is easier to read than the Western one. One can see the various village-units that make up the town-units; one can understand how these amalgamate into the city itself.

In the American city, unless one understands the complicated social and economic forces involved, one cannot understand why the main shopping districts should be moved from the centre to the suburbs, why this ring city should have no central section, why there is little public transportation to such distant areas. The Western city is the more civilized in that it is the more highly evolved, maybe more efficient but certainly more difficult to understand and more uncomfortable to live in. Its assumptions are quite different.

A Western surmise is that a city should be logically planned and built to last. Each structure is presumed to be in its proper place and constructed to endure. It is believed that what a person builds will be enjoyed by his or her descendents. The urban complex may be enhanced, individual buildings may be replaced, the structure itself may be altered, but the assumption remains that, once built, it will remain intrinsically as it was. This is accepted as literally true, and the architect correspondingly builds for the future.

An Eastern assumption, seen especially in the cities of Japan and particularly in its capital, is quite different. The city is not planned, and its buildings are subject to almost routine renewal. Opportunities to redesign the city – earthquakes, fires, wartime bombings – are ignored, and solid buildings younger than those who live in them are pulled down to make way for new ones. The assumption is that the city itself is transient, and the architect consequently builds for the present.

The Western city assumes immortality. Buildings are made to last. Behind this somewhat illogical notion – since human beings and their works are nothing if not mortal – lies another concept. This is that one somehow ought at least to appear immortal in one's edifices: anything which is made should be made for the ages.

This in turn implies some amount of striving. The architecture reaches for something more than the human – think of the soaring Gothic style. Dissatisfied with the common state of limited mortality, the Westerner makes architectural attempts to deny it. (As indeed do the more official cities of the East – Beijing is as solid as the Pyramids, but in the Chinese countryside peasants continue to build in mortal clay.) This denial is responsible for some architectural wonders, but it is also responsible for decaying New York.

Asians, particularly the Japanese, have not (or have not until recently) shared such assumptions. Rather, their assumptions have been just the opposite. Impermanence is acknowledged as the natural state and transience as a prime quality of life. There is constant sameness within constant change, and it is this quality that creates what small permanence the Japanese observe.

Take the great shrine at Ise, Shinto's Vatican, located in a cryptomeria forest near Matsuzaka. It is torn down once every twenty years. The large wooden structure is demolished, and a replica – identical in all respects – is constructed adjacent to it. Two decades later, when the new building becomes old, it too is destroyed and a structure precisely similiar is erected on the land the older building formerly occupied. This has been going on for centuries and indicates Japan's accommodating answer to the demands of immortality.

The Japanese city follows the same pattern. For this reason, Tokyo seems always to be under construction. Indeed, it will never be finished. One thinks of Calvino's city of Thekla, a place always being constructed: 'If you ask, "Why is Thekla's construction taking such a long time?" the inhabitants continue hoisting sacks, lowering leaded strings . . . as they answer, "So that its destruction cannot begin."'

The logic of the Japanese city lies in just this temporal consideration. Its assumption (so unlike those of the Western city, which seems to live entirely in its past) is that 'now' is important, but 'now' lies well within the framework of the accepted concept of permanence-within-continual-change. Tokyo's buildings are consequently always new and yet, in this sense, always the same.

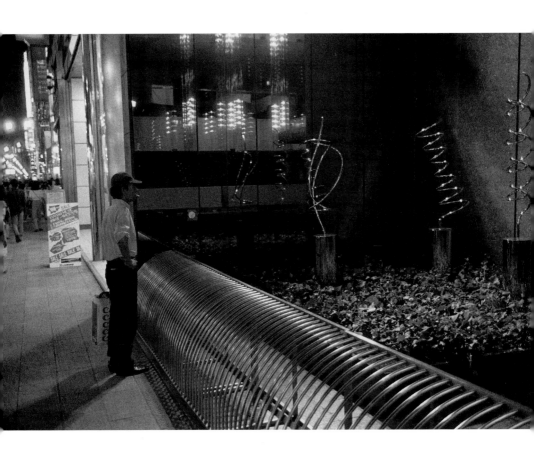

Which kind of city best suits human beings is a question that must be answered individually. Certainly, Tokyo with its villages and towns inside the central city, its convenience, its very non-centralization, fits a society where the family and other social units remain important. At the same time, its systems of public transportation make travelling from one section of this enormous city to another both possible and comfortable. Tokyo is one of the few major cities where one does not want to own a car.

At the same time, Tokyo would seem to lack those architectural monuments which speak so eloquently of timelessness, of immortality, except, as we have seen, in the very concept of timeless impermanence that the Japanese city has incorporated into itself.

Western visitors are thus presented with an anomaly when they visit a city such as Tokyo. They cannot detect the natural and organic form of the city because structural logic has no place in such a form, yet they find an anthropomorphosed city in that the more-than-human is unstressed and the merely human is emphasized.

Nor is Tokyo, despite its seeming modernity, a city that makes Western assumptions. That one often cannot locate an address without outside (police, postman, local resident) help would indicate that it is not in any Western sense an efficient urban complex. As D. J. Enright wisely remarked, though in another context, 'Ambiguity interests the Japanese a good deal more than does logic.'

Indeed, much is illogical and inefficient. Kurt Singer, speaking of the Japanese language, noticed that it is so rich in ambiguities that '. . . nobody deplores the resulting measure of haziness. It is by higher degrees of clarity and precision that the Japanese would feel inconvenienced.'

But then, logical efficiency as a noble virtue is not a Japanese concept. Rather, efficiency is mundanely humanized. So is logic. Conflicts, for example, are not battled out. They are eschewed: 'Conflicting powers [Singer again] are reduced to ceremonial forms allocated to well-defined places and times and occasions.'

Illogical, inefficient Tokyo will seem, despite initial strangeness, somehow familiar, as visitors discover if they stay long enough.

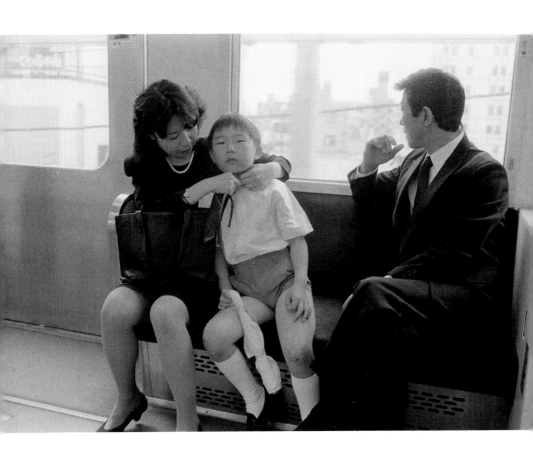

They may realize that its pattern is that of their own home-towns, if they come from a home-town small enough.

Each one of these small units from which this large city is made is indeed a town. It feels like one. It acts like one.

10 March 1960. I go to my neighbourhood bath and stay a long time. I am very fond of it; it is the nearest thing to church, to the barber's, to a family.

They are all more or less alike, these baths, one to every neighbourhood, there must be thousands in Tokyo: a large barn-like building, tall chimney attached which begins smoking about two in the afternoon and continues to midnight. Inside, the building is divided into four equal-sized rooms. The back two (the baths) have a half-wall between; front two have a partition with a bath for the woman in charge so she can survey both sides (men's and women's) at the same time. The clothes are left in large baskets. Pay the money to the girl, sixteen yen; shampoo or a razor are five yen each; usually carry your own soap and towel.

Most of the bathers hold their towels in front of them when they go in; a habitual gesture; you see the same gesture in fully dressed men when they are cold; they cover their genitals. Originally I thought it was because of the girls working around but it is not. They pay no attention to the men nor the men to them. This is the country of the time and place for everything and the bath is not the place for sex.

Foreigners are told that they must wash outside the big tile baths, using the taps and little wooden buckets, and then get in. Well, maybe foreigners do but the Japanese certainly don't. On cold nights, like tonight, they climb in all dirty and let the communal water soak it off. At best the tap rinse is a mere token: feet, hands, maybe balls, but not often.

Everyone says the Japanese aren't dirty, that they are in fact clean. Well, I suppose they are cleaner than many, but no Japanese that I know bathes because he likes it. He bathes to get warm usually (once out and covered up, the body heat remains

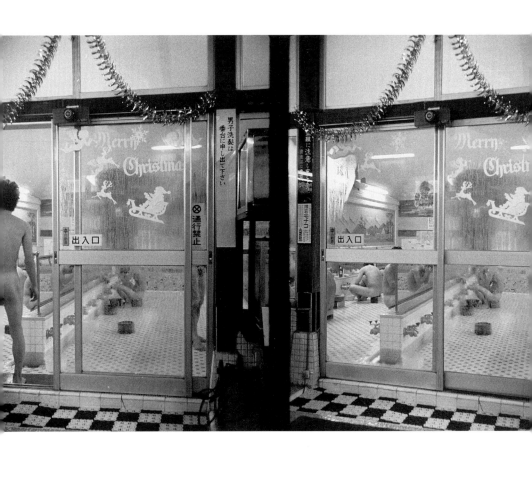

for the water is scalding) and he bathes to meet his friends. But not, I think, to get any cleaner than anyone else. Certainly not many bathe completely. Most men don't skin back and wash; and I have been told that women think it is immodest to get soap up inside. Once the bath is over, too, the dirty underwear goes right back on.

But it is nice in the bath and that is quite enough. You sit back and scald. It is relaxing. Perhaps that is why, in the bath and turning lobster-red, Japanese will say things they would otherwise not. Perhaps this is why one can always hear neighbourhood gossip in the bath.

One sits back in water which doesn't feel as dirty as it is only because it is so hot, looks at the picture (all bathhouses have one, a giant mural against the back wall, sometimes Western-type scenes, castle and sailboat and deer, sometimes a Chinese palace, not a Japanese castle in sight: all oil on tin and mildew), reads the advertisements (Love Beauty Salon, Suzuki's Expert TV Repair, Fame Barber Shop), and listens to the gossip.

Today I learn that that nice Mrs Watanabe down the street doesn't know that that nice Mr Watanabe – glasses and a wen – is keeping a girl young enough to be his daughter. Also learn that the eldest Hamada boy (much given to body building, has a bulging neck) is going to be the death of his parents, plays around with girls, and him so careful of his body too. Then someone says that if he had Mrs Watanabe around he'd keep *two* girls; another, that with parents like that he wonders the Hamada boy hadn't run away years ago.

Maybe if I hadn't been there I too would have had a defender the day my grocer turned to a neighbour and said: 'And that foreigner, the one with all the hair; you know he never pulls down the blinds . . . well, the other night' – but just then he saw me bending forward with interest. I wanted to find out what had happened just the other night but he sank deeper into the hot water until just his eyes showed.

Once out of the tub then everyone washes (my soap at present is Chlorophyll Cow) using skeleton of sponge and a kind of pumice stone on the hands and feet. My towel has naked ladies on it which is always good for a conversation or two.

Here the attitude towards sex is representative. No people have it more firmly in place. They are a bit puritan sometimes, and a number of prudes exist, but there is no people less prurient. What they *are* prurient about is money. Some Japanese treat money as we treat sex. But, as for sex – well, there are no young bloods trying to peek over the partition.

Talk to a number of people this evening. One old man says: 'Say, there's something I've been wanting to ask you. Are there lots of Indians left? Hear you've been having some trouble with them.' But it turns out he thought Indians and Negroes were the same thing. A little child comes up and spits water at me, then I remember that sometime back I taught him how to squirt it with his hands. Can't use his hands properly and so the inventive child uses his mouth.

While strolling the streets of the city, descending as it were into its various sections, the large towns within the city – Asakusa, Ueno, Ginza, Shinjuku – let us for a moment search out the old, what is left of it, to sense it as W. E. Griffes did when he first saw the city in 1870:

> To feel that for ages millions . . . have lived and loved, enjoyed and suffered and died, living the fullness of life, yet without the religion, laws, customs, food, dress and culture which seems to us to be the virtuals of our social existence, is like walking through a living Pompeii.

Of buildings, very few – none I think from Tokugawa times except for the Toshogu Shrine in Ueno, left over from 1650, and a small temple or two now occupying a gentrified little park beside the Asakusa Kannon Temple. Nor would one expect many such remains, not with the many fires, earthquakes and bombings of this century.

At the same time, there are definite remains of another sort. The architect Maki Fumihiko has demonstrated how contemporary Tokyo retains a surprising amount of its nineteenth-century Edo

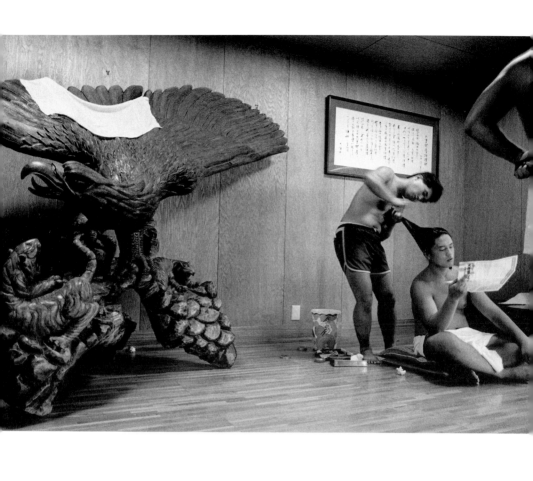

framework. The pattern of roads remains basically unchanged, and the groups of self-contained 'towns' – conforming to the city's topography – remain true to their Edo-period antecedents.

Edward Seidensticker has said that the High City changed less than the Low City, that class distinctions, once very clear if measured by money, tended to disappear from the Low City but remained in the High City. So also to a remarkable extent did the pattern of land usage, the distribution of property between the affluent and the more straitened: 'In both parts of the city the street pattern, despite revolution and disaster, has continued to resemble that of Edo.'

Jinnai Hidenobu, in his 'spatial anthropology' of Tokyo, found that new forms were reset on inherited space and 'developed as a modern city squarely atop this old structure . . . the essential features of Edo urban forms passed on unaltered'. And Tange Kenzo, creator of Tokyo's most extreme modern building, the *Metropolis*-like City Hall in Shinjuku, believes that '. . . everywhere you go in Tokyo, traditions and preferences of past generations – particularly those of the Edo period – exist side by side with the Japanese preference for the avant garde and whatever is chic.'

Tokyo, then, follows its old ways. So do many cities. London, for example. After the fire of 1666, at least six city plans (including one by Christopher Wren and another by John Evelyn) were produced and none were used, at least not by London. One of them ended up becoming Philadelphia, and Major Pierre l'Enfant's plan for Washington owed much to Wren's for London.

As Nikolaus Pevsner noted, the 'failure' of Wren and the other planners meant that London still follows its medieval (even Saxon) street patterns. As does Tokyo. And in the sinuous curving of Tokyo's elevated highway system, one may still trace the routes of vanished streams and moats.

A difference is that, unlike London or Paris, early nineteenth-century Tokyo had much open space. These park-like enclosures were often the estates of the various daimyo, and, when the Tokugawa regime at last collapsed, they became government property to be turned over or sold to private owners. Both the New Otani and the Akasaka Prince hotels occupy hilltop daimyo estates; most of the Tokyo university campuses are from daimyo or upper-level samurai property. In a remarkably short time, all of these areas were filled up, and Tokyo remains a city with very little open park space – though it has more than even more crammed Osaka.

Searchers for the old in Tokyo will thus discover some battered evidence. One such remain, now so compromised that it might be considered a paradigm, is Nihombashi, the Nippon Bridge. This structure, located along the upper stretches of what is now the Ginza, was originally so important a place that all distances in Japan were measured from it. It retained this importance until the age of the automobile, which in Japan began well after the Second World War. One may now view the melancholy but instructive results.

The bridge must be read as geological strata. At the bottom is what is left of the canal which the structure bridges. Once a small river, it is now channelled and straightened and forgotten. Somewhere down there are the stone ponts of the Edo-period bridge. On top of these, still visible, is the 1911 bridge, cast metal with ornamental unicorns and 'Korean' dogs (metaphors for West and East) sitting around its lampposts. Over it all roars the present century, an elevated highway which misses the heraldic beasts by mere metres and renders the bridge all but invisible in the sense that no-one notices it, eclipsed as it is by the vaunting of the overhead traffic. It is, in the archaeological sense, a remain: an historical sandwich.

To this extent, then, Edo remains visible – in the bone structure and, occasionally, in a petrified protrusion like Nihonbashi. Tradition is more visible in other areas of endeavour – in food, the language, in attitudes – and there is enough of it that one may still agree with George Curzon's 75-year-old definition of Japan as 'a country of feverish proficiency in many of the habits of advanced civilizations with uncompromising relics of feudal crystalization'. Except that Japan is itself now 'advanced'.

In fact, it is so 'advanced' that Tokyo has become one of the most spectacular of modern cities in that it appears much more 'modern'

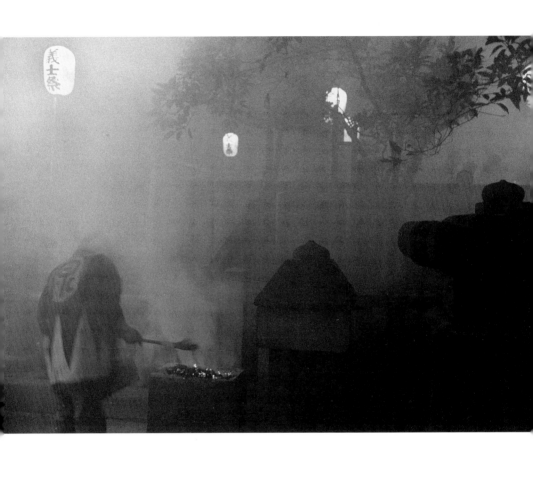

than Paris, London or even Las Vegas. We have seen why this should be so; we will now look at some of the results. First, however, some opinion.

Despite the fact that most Japanese seem to want to live in Tokyo, not all of them have a high opinion of the place. This coolness began quite early, around 1021, when the Lady Sarashina described crossing the Sumida in her diary, on her way back to Kyoto. 'We are in Musashi [where Edo was to be located],' she wrote, 'a province without a single charming place to recommend it.' In the early 1920s, Kafu visited the Musashi suburbs and found 'a jumble of houses for rent and little factories, packed in quite without order – the unsightliness is even worse than the worst parts of the city proper'.

And in Tanizaki's *The Makioka Sisters*, one of the sisters goes to Second-World-War Tokyo and believes that after Osaka or Kyoto it looks like 'a rude, unfinished frontier community' somewhere further north, 'or even Manchuria'.

Tanizaki's quarrel with Tokyo was well known. In *Diary of a Mad Old Man*, he has his protagonist say of the post-war city (in Howard Hibbett's translation):

> I don't like the Tokyo of today . . . Who made Tokyo into such a miserable, chaotic city? Weren't they all boorish, country-bred politicians unaware of the good qualities of old Tokyo? Weren't those the men who turned our beautiful canals into muddy ditches, men who never knew that whitebait swam in the Sumida River.

Foreign observers have often been critical of Tokyo as well, whatever the era of their visit. In this they have subscribed to a hostility to cities in general that was formed in the West early on. There have been numerous city haters, including William Morris, Oswald Spengler, Friedrich Engels and George Orwell. City lovers have tended to give places bad names as well – witness Walt Whitman's effusive discovery that New York was 'a continued exaltation and absolute fulfillment'. A more temperate urban view was that of Lewis Mumford. He saw 'sprawl and shapelessness as an inevitable by product of immensity', but then went on to suggest that sprawl and immensity were not entirely undesirable.

An early visitor to Japan, Isabella Bird, would have had none of that. Noting that the country's highest creed consisted of bald materialism – 'material good its goal' – she went on to observe: 'It is singular that the Japanese who rarely commit a solecism in their own national costume, architecture or decorative arts, seem to be perfectly destitute of perception when they borrow ours.'

Japan's sprawl was rendered even more ugly in that it was not even Japanese sprawl. It was an imitated Western sprawl. Henry Norman heard a diplomat say, 'Japan, you see, is a bad translation.' Later still, Lincoln Steffins wrote: 'Sometimes it looks as if Japan were created as a satire on and for Western civilization.'

An implication of this is that modern Japan is in bad taste. Without enquiring too closely into the foundations of that agreement known as good taste, one can say that a known kind of bad taste clearly proliferates. This is of the sort which the West calls kitsch.

Indeed, Japan is a kingdom of kitsch and Tokyo is its kapital. Mt Fuji ends up as a tissue dispenser, and the Buddha's sandals – three metres high – adorn a ferro-concrete temple pretending to be timber. Here the food in restaurant windows, more mouth-watering than real food, is made of plastic; here the Fontana de Trevi in plaster fronts a designer-elevator high-rise; here record shops soberly sell a CD transcription of *Le Sacre du printemps* for solo guitar.

These objects all have kitsch in common. The dictionary offers that the term derives from *kitschen* (1860), 'to cheapen', and a later authority says that its attributes invariably include an adaptation from one medium to another: wood-imitation wallpaper, the 'convenience' hotel built to resemble Windsor Castle; Tomita's synthesized 'edition' of Ravel's *Daphnis and Chloe*. Another quality, it is said, is that kitsch always represents an effort to diminish scale and reduce functional activities to domestic terms – as in the Fuji tissue dispenser.

But to cheapen also means to make more economical. Making small, making standard, indeed making in traditional Japanese

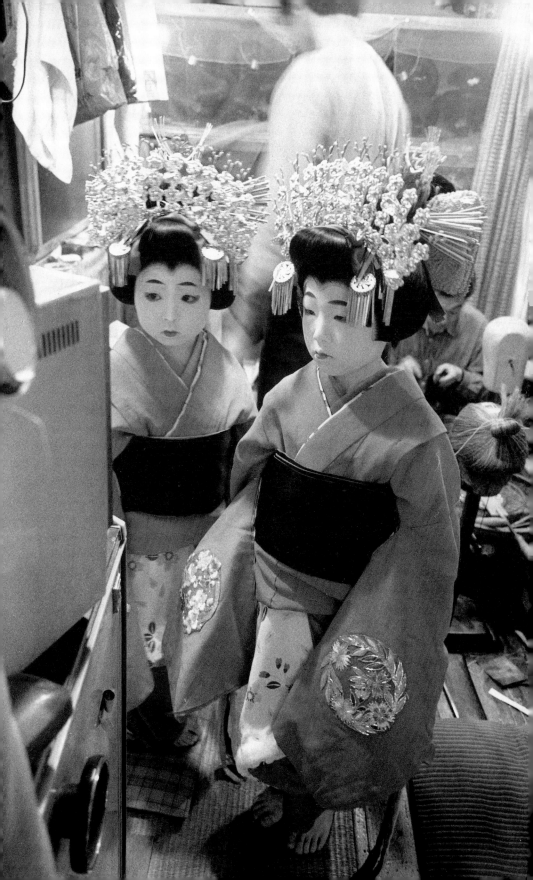

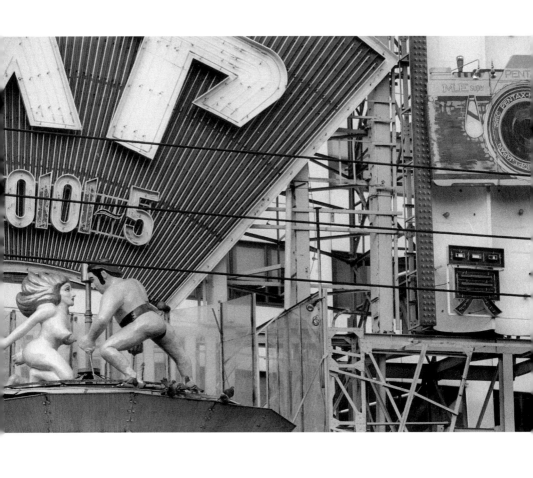

style. Tatami mats, shoji doors, always in predetermined sizes, created affordable Japanese architecture; microchips, always in modular sizes, now create affordable Japanese electronics. And Japanese digital technology now makes things even smaller.

In this most pragmatic of nations, everything must be for immediate use. Architecturally, this means that a pure style (if there is any such) would be too limiting (in terms of time, space and energy) for domestic use. How much more practical to miniaturize, to diversify, to combine. More information in less space, as on a silicon chip.

That any original integrity has been violated is no-one's concern, nor is the fact that the result is often kitschy. Indeed, the Japanese language has no word for kitsch. Nor would one expect it to. To quote an old Japanese proverb, 'Fish have no word for water.'

Thus modern Tokyo is a glorious architectural confusion of plastic tile and fake wood, of Corinthian columns and chrome pylons, dormer windows and polarized glass, half-timber and red-brick paste-on fronting, sheet steel, translucent paper, textured lucite. Any precision of architectural message is of course lost, though the results are impressively loud.

Loud though it may be, the message is garbled, because neither Japanese sender nor Japanese receiver can read it. A Tokyo person cannot know the nexus that contributes the meaning of the Massachusetts dormer window any more than a New Yorker can hold that mass of recollection which makes a shrine's torii gateway meaningful.

Brass ivy adorning fake New Orleans fretwork; a monster stadium disguised as a Big Egg; a plastic advertising gorilla wearing the Stars and Stripes; a wedding cake of a building selling bridal costumes; lots of big roof-top Venuses de Milo and Statues of Liberty. Their statements are unintelligible, but they are also disarming, diverting and even, if you squint, witty. Also, they are resolutely modern.

In fact, that is what this mélange says, its single intelligible statement: 'I am modern.' This is because the world at large is, in this late Hellenistic time of ours, enamoured of kitsch. Call it post-modernism or what you will; it has become artistically respectable. A taste for kitsch is a taste for the times.

This was foreseen by an eminent observer, the novelist Hermann Broch, who, back in 1933, stated that '. . . all periods in which values decline are kitsch periods.' However, he was not thinking of Japan nor could he have been, because in this area Japan had no standards from which to decline.

Though there *were* standards in traditional Japan, there were never standards for foreign imports. As Percival Lowell recognized over a century ago, '. . . the Japanese have been a nation of importers, not of merchandize, but of ideas.' In its importing of attitudes, Japan was avant-garde, as it were, in its early appreciation of foreign kitsch. For example, it recognized early on the beauty and utility of that nineteenth-century Belgian import, the *Manneke Pis*. This attractive youngster now relieves himself in most Japanese cities, usually in the form of a public fountain and often with an ensemble of appropriate costumes changes, all respectably civic in intention – a fireman's uniform, a policeman's uniform.

Now, of course, traditional taste itself, unintelligible to the young, has been crafted into something new. These dead canons are the basis of the 'Japanesque', in itself a newer sub-species of kitsch. Holy sutras are printed in gold on neckties, one enters the latest disco through a chrome torii gateway, and Seibu's Roppongi Wave Building has a holograph image of Jizo, a Buddhist patron.

The confusion of styles that is typical of po-mo kitsch allows one to nullify the other. It is like a *pousse-café*, a rainbow of tastelessness. There is no single flavour. Wandering in a smart Tokyo neighborhood is like wandering in a box of Quality Street: everything is different, everything tastes the same.

Which leads us to fashion, a phenomenon which, as Walter Benjamin has told us, describes 'the ritual by which the fetish Commodity wishes to be worshipped'.

It is fitting, perhaps inevitable, that Japan should become associated with high fashion. One reason is that the country has always been aware of the kind of transience that fashion emphasizes; another is that novelty for its own sake has never been unfashionable. Still another is that after Japan's long, enforced historical

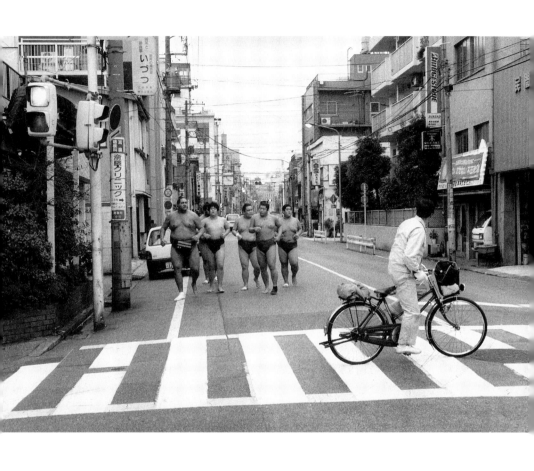

seclusion (fell asleep under Elizabeth, woke up under Victoria, people used to say), the public went wild for newness. That something is new is recommendation enough; that it is new and on sale is an enormous incentive – as witness the cries of '*shin hatsubai*' (latest product) on street and TV.

Edward Seidensticker has given us a listing of some Meiji fads. These included, besides coffee and sea-bathing, a number of animal fashions, among which was a passion for pigs, including the miniature variety known as Nanking mice, and a major vogue for rabbits, particularly calico ones. This continued until '. . . a person in Shitaya was fined and jailed for staining a white rabbit with persimmon juice.'

In a way, the animal passion continues. Just last year, the stores were awash with *tamagotchi*: a virtual pet in the form of a compact, portable computer game shaped like an egg (*tamago*) that one 'watched' (*gotchi* being a kind of homonym for the English word.) The instructions read: 'You take care of Tamagotchi, the mysterious small animal on the liquid crystal screen. The special feature is that Tamagotchi will grow up in diverse ways, depending on how you raise it.'

The computer image of an egg gave birth five seconds after a button was pushed. The creature had a life expectancy of a week or so and during this time constantly called for attention by means of a beeping sound. The owner was required to feed it, to dispose of its excrement, to play with it and to discipline it – all by pushing various buttons. Its appearance and character were affected by the degree of care it received. If not fed enough, it died of starvation; if ignored, it turned delinquent. There were ways to make it old (an *oyajichi*, displaying features of the middle-aged), and it could always be reprogrammed to start all over again. There were Internet pages that offered advice on how to make it reach an advanced age (discipline it and feed it less, no matter how much it complains); there was also dissident advice on how to kill the thing as quickly and efficiently as possible.

Invented by a toy manufacturer who was pondering the mingling of pets with toys, Tamagotchi became popular at once. Released at the end of 1996, it sold millions of units and half a year later was still being eagerly awaited by would-be buyers. These were initially teenage girls, but eventually included everyone.

As an image, the Tamagotchi displayed differences from its parents – digital games. It was not entirely presentational; it presumed a dialogue. The cute little encoded avians had to be cared for. This, said some educators (as well as the Bandai Co. Ltd, which makes the product), was a good thing. In the cities, the young are not allowed pets; they do not learn the interdependence so necessary for a healthy society. Tamagotchi teaches them responsibility.

Some owners, it was said optimistically, developed a parental attachment to the chick that was as deep as that towards human offspring. On television, a doctor – a grown man – said that when his Tamagotchi passed away he was sadder than when one of his patients died. An Internet home page displayed illustrations of Tamagotchi tombstones and invited people to send valedictions to be engraved on them.

There were other reasons for the product's popularity, however. Teenagers in all countries are notoriously under-empowered; their entire culture is about ways to acquire adult power before their time. With the tiny chick, they finally had something completely under their thumbs. It survived based on decisions they made; it died at their whim: indeed, it lived the kind of life they thought they did, but it could do nothing about it. They could. They had Tamagotchi.

That Tamagotchi became a craze is perhaps also indicative of something other than mere popularity. In Japan more than in some countries, everyone is supposed to look the same. If a new fashion evolves (*chapatsu* – dyed hair; loose socks worn by girls; Burberry scarves; *puri-cura* – print club, tiny stickers of one and one's friends, all beaming and holding up V-sign fingers), then you are out if you do not have it. But even if you have it, there are crazes inside the crazes. It was only the white Tamagotchi which (like the calico rabbit) really counted.

What is newer than fashion itself? Clothes. Fashion is the essence of modernity, the only essence it owns. Take it away and we have clothing, not fashion.

Another reason for the attention paid to high fashion is that Japan standardizes radically. People tend to look alike (one hair colour, unless it is dyed; only two eye colours, brown and black), and so their natural appearance does not exhibit the physical diversity seen in some Western countries. This is turned into a virtue, and people dress alike as well: the navy-blue business suit, the high-collared or middy-bloused school uniform, the occupational clothes.

Fashionable clothing is thus a new uniform. Everyone wears the same things, but the things themselves differ according to season or designer whim. Last year, all fashionable youngsters had to wear black, but only for a time; after that it was pastels: lilac, beige, putty. This year, it's something else.

One point is that all of this is new. Another is that everyone is wearing it. One point does not cancel out the other because, in its small way, each new fashion is also a protest. The latest thing, even when worn by everyone at the same time, registers a small criticism of whatever they all wore before. This sort of small protest is the kind of criticism most popular in Japan. It is safe and yet, for a brief time, lends a feeling of individuality.

Naturally, individuality is felt as strongly in Japan as elsewhere – it is simply that it is expressed less directly. In a country moulded by the group (three centuries of Tokugawa rule saw to that), individuals are expected to conform (unless they're modern architects, those token individuals), and so they often do. Thus does one satisfy the demands of the social order.

Many Japanese find freedom in crowds because being anonymous is one way of achieving respite from the restraints of this social order. Streets are often narrow, always crowded: Shinjuku at night is New Year's Eve anywhere else. To be a part of any group is to be similar, and in Japan similarity is agreed upon as a virtue, as it is in any feudal society. Despite surface democratization, many Japanese are not particularly friendly to the idea of the individual,

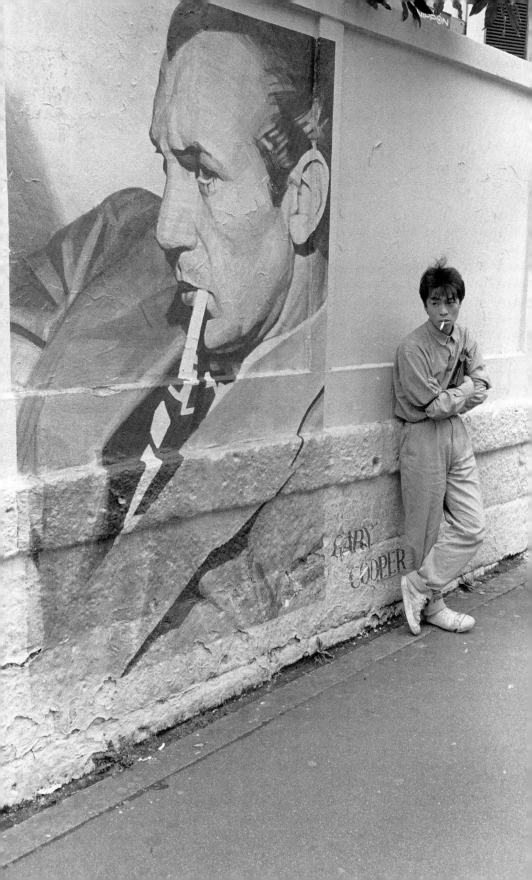

as least not to ideal individuals, as Americans are purported to be. This is reflected in the shape of the city itself, in the architectural patterns of the country.

Kurt Singer observed that many (in his time, the 1930s, most) Japanese learn to move 'within a tightening set of restrictive rules' which usually provide them with a structure. Western 'freedom for' finds its equivalent in 'constraint for', and the resulting individual is built to a common cut more openly and more often than is thought usual in the West. This self-constructed 'self', which is all that any of us can boast of by way of 'personality', seems, by contrast, muted.

As it would if everyone wore the same thing, said the same thing and, for all we know, thought the same thing. But none of this is so; it is just that the majority make it seem so. Japanese individuals express an individuality less apparent. One of the ways they do this is through what they wear, and as we have seen one of the attractions of high fashion is that a statement of assent can be read as a statement of criticism as well as a celebration of togetherness.

Let us look at a few of these fleeting fashions through extracts from my journals:

September 22, 1992. I notice a change in women's fashion, now that fashion is ordained not only by the media, but by women themselves. The ones I see are developing a new style. It consists of more expensive materials arranged in more expensive ways. Silks and velvets tucked and pleated, a torso swathed and looped. These things cost money and are commensurate with the new economic strength. I recall that when the West was consolidating its financial position at the end of the last century women's clothing turned into expensive upholstery, labour intensive.

There is something else as well. The women are turning into royalty. There is a lot of inset embroidery, gold plate, tassels and cords, with crowns stitched onto the material. This makes the women a bit overdressed as they buy eggs and tofu in my neighbourhood supermarket. There is also a smart turn to the military look – epaulets, aide-de-camp ribbon effects. I do not find this

74

sinister. It is a part of the look of royalty, of new power. All of this is seen only in middle-class women, all of them now dressed in a particularly recognizable form of bad taste, the overtly ostentatious. (The *covertly* ostentatious forms a different kind of bad taste, that which is called good.) The further taste of the wealthy and the fashion-conscious is different yet, it is still Issey Miyake body bags and Comme des Garçons shrouds.

July, 7 1994. I look at summer fashions of the young. Those of the male are most curious. Big heavy leather laced shoes, clod-hoppers, have taken the place of last winter's big heavy laced track shoes. The shorts are of heavy jersey, with great wide leg openings and consequent panoramas of thigh. With this is worn a lettered T-shirt – one with an algebraic formula, another in the Cyrillic alphabet, yet another, worn by a fresh-faced innocent, with 'I Am a Pervert' on the back. Or the outfit consists of a ragged dress shirt held together with safety pins and jeans which have been carefully ripped at the knees suggesting some strenuous labour which has, in fact, not been undertaken. All of these soft-skinned kids are strangers to work. Their outfits cost money and came from Harajuku. They are affecting the proletariat.

This, says Veblen, occurs where money seeps far down, accompanied by a like decline in standards. Romans in full fashion dressing like Goths. All of this shabby finery looks strange in Ueno, however, where the fashionable young must compete with the real thing – bums with the knees of their pants honourably worn through, homeless old women actually needing to safety-pin their blouses.

December 15 , 1996. I wander around and look at the girls in their Frankenstein boots and their elephant sox, and the boys under their variously coloured thatch – blue is popular right now. I also listen to people talking on their cellular phones . . . these focus all attention in the ears rather than, as is customary on the street, in the eyes. The users do not realize that they are spilling their lives into the ears of the passers-by and if they did they would not care.

I loiter near to hear what they are saying. They pay no attention.

Besides, if they do notice, they see merely a foreigner and foreigners are famous for not knowing the language. So I feel like Siegfried in the forest – understanding the language of the birds.

But this promiscuous telephoning can be dangerous. Last night's news told of a man using his phone on the platform as the express rushed by. He was so intent on what he was saying that he walked too close to the hurtling train, was drawn into it and sucked onto the tracks where he made his final connection.

December 24, 1996. I walk the windy streets of Shibuya, a territory now given over to the young. There they come in their hordes, driven by fashion and their glands. Let me describe them lest this motley show be lost forever.

Younger high-school girls wear their plaid skirts and sweaters and their elephants sox, loose, baggy, white, which they say makes their legs look thinner and often have to be held up with a kind of glue which is especially made and sold over the counter. They still sometimes wear old-fashioned braids but their manners have been attuned to the times. In particular they cultivate a loud, braying, humourless laugh which is supposed to indicate a lack of docility. Among themselves they use male language mistaking this for a kind of emancipation.

Older girls often wear very short skirts coupled with built-up boots which reach the knee and thus offer an expanse of leg. With this a long overcoat unbuttoned so that the thighs may flash. Long dyed hair (chestnut, maple, mahogany) or streaked with peroxide or henna, and brown pancake make-up with silvered lipstick complete the ensemble.

It has a name. It is called *kogaru* – derived apparently from *kokosei garu* (high-school girl), though the layered cut, the trimmed eyebrows and the lipstick emulate the image of the older popular singer Namie Amuro. Some of the girls show their navels in the summer and often sport a ring in them.

Full piercing is seen mainly on the boys. Those in high school wear eyebrow studs or lip studs as well as earrings. This with jeans and lumberjack shirts (now firmly at the waist since the pubic-hair-showing groin-look is out of fashion) and boots with

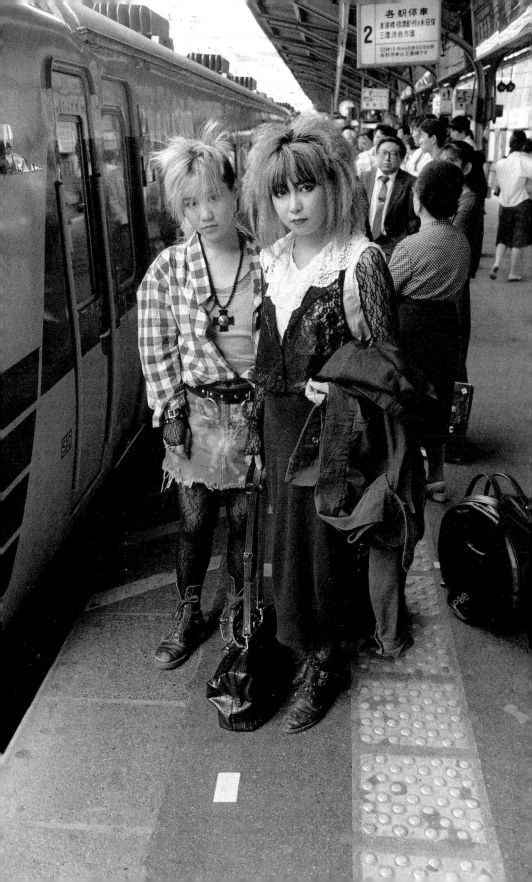

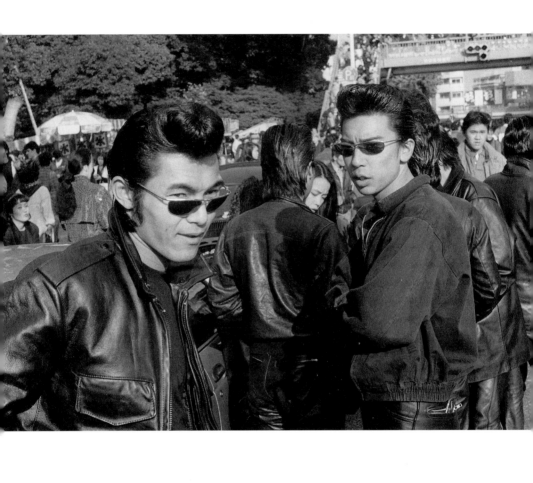

thick soles, and lots of rings. Boys in Shibuya are more decorated than the girls are.

Along with this a new vocabulary. *Saiko* and *saitei* for best and worst are out. In is *choberiba* for very bad and *choberigu* for very good. I do not know the derivation of these. Another new word is *makudurama* which can mean anything from a big sports event to a big rock concert to a big TV spectacular. Continuing into the new year is a teenage passion for *purikura*, photo stickers made in three minutes showing you and your friend wearing funny hats, grinning, making the V-sign, with which you can decorate your school locker or your letters, if you send any.

Back in Ueno, only twenty minutes on the subway, is another world. Here the young are more scarce and are not overly given to body piercing nor wearing work clothes as a fashion indicator. Here the work clothes are seen on the working young, but mainly on people who are older, and poorer. Much less shopping going on. In the station lines of old men, indigent, homeless, sitting on the pavement. I pass two in noisy conversation. One drunkenly tells the other: '*Issen mo nai'n da yo*' (I don't have a penny), yet he must have had at least several to get this drunk.

15 March, 1997. I come back late from teaching my class and find the back streets of Ueno awash with beautiful young women, all in the epaulets and monograms, brocades and miniskirts that signify the *mizushobai* service, all from bars named Etoile and Hope which cost an amount of money. Money is now not to be had, however, and so they have come outside, like exotic insects from under their rocks, and – very ill at ease in their indoor finery – stand in the open night air, hand out leaflets and cajole.

They are joined by the homeless who are bedding down for the night, on cardboard in front of banks, or curled up in the little niche by the porno. A piquant combination: long tanned legs next to dirty shoes and sockless feet; much-brushed hair, stained fashionable mahogony or deep maple side by side with dirty, lank, infested strands; the smell of Chanel mingling with that of the rotgut the homeless take to put themselves to sleep.

79

June 9, 1997. A sunny, summer Sunday, lots of people out in the city, including the new breed: the nubile moneyed. They are there in designer duds (Ralph Lauren is favoured), loose white sox, pleated miniskirts, if they are still students; if not, platform shoes, frosty lipstick, streaked dyed hair (brown), no more Vuitton bags, Fendi now. They stroll in groups buying things. Tamagotchi is now *de trop*, since they are selling them at supermarkets, so everyone has one and the fad is over. But Print Club (a digital camera machine which makes multiple tiny snapshots of them and their friends) is still in. Perhaps this is because the company which makes the machine, Atlas, has also emblazoned its slogan: 'People with lots of our photos are happiest, but people who aren't popular cannot collect many.' Therefore, those with most of these photos are most popular and hence happiest. To show how happy they are these young women have cultivated a deep, loud, mirthless laugh which is used constantly, and have amplified ordinary noise-making into something like menace. You can hear them coming.

One way to read all this is by what is not there – that is, males. All this is something for girls to do now that boys are hopeless: they are all tied up with expectations (the job), they are zombied out (video games, porn tapes), they can't talk, they can't think, they just aren't much fun. But we girls, we know how to have fun: we giggle, we scream, we have our pictures taken by the hundreds, we shop – here we come.

As one gathers, fashion is not only clothing, but clothing is only fashion. Also one sees a certain consistency. Just as the *iki*, the truly chic, in Edo were centred around the whorehouse (dignified by other terminology but a whorehouse nonetheless) – what they wore, what you wore, what they talked about, what you talked about – so the new *kogaru* fashion was brought to prominence by the activities of these high-school girls, some of whom also engaged in *enjo kosai*, a term that has been euphemistically translated as 'compensated dates'.

Style is how you express yourself, how you say things, how you present the real you. Rémy de Gourmont once said that trying to define style was like trying to put a sack of flour in a thimble, but another Frenchman, André Bazin, suggested that it was more simple: style was a pattern of selection, and what you chose was what you were.

In the case of cities, the chosen pattern is often contradictory. Rome's is a combination of the ancient (Imperial Rome) and the more recently elegant (Armani, Valentino, Gucci); London's is a combination of probity (the House of Lords, Westminster Abbey) and trendy ('swinging-city' punk). Tokyo style is also a combination of opposites.

Tokyo's self-identification is exemplified by 'trad but mod', the city's ubiquitous slogan found on shop-fronts, T-shirts and carrier bags. The capital insists on its traditions: a few early nineteenth-century Edo-period buildings, the Imperial Palace, the more and more gentrified Low City. 'Established in 1995' is carved in granite on a recent emporium. At the same time, as five minutes in the city will convince you, Tokyo insists on its modernity.

It always has. For a century now, Tokyo had been known as the 'city of contrasts' or the 'capital of the old and the new'. Ever since its opening up to the outside world in the middle of the last century, Tokyo has with increasing skill combined East and West, past and present.

The case is complicated, however, because Japan has long been 'modern' in that it was largely responsible for the international modern style. Architect Richard Rogers, the man liable for Paris's Centre Pompidou, has said that the whole modern movement sprang directly from architects 'looking at things like the Katsura Detached Palace' – an example of Japanese architecture at its most geometric. And the poet Henri Michaux, in Tokyo in 1932, noted that 'the Japanese have been modern for ten centuries,' that '. . . Tokyo is a hundred times more modern than Paris.'

When the Russian film director Andrei Tarkovsky wanted a city of the future in *Solaris,* he brought his camera to Tokyo's Akasaka-Mitsuke. Ridley Scott's Los Angeles of the future in *Blade Runner* was conceived after the director had seen night-time Shinjuku.

The air of the new in Tokyo is, in addition (unlike that in the Scott film), benign. Contented people walk about wearing Discman earphones; they use plastic cards for just about everything; they wait for traffic lights. And it all works: public phones are never out of order, automatic dispensers (beer, saké, soft drinks, magazines, condoms, sandwiches, hot dinners) actually dispense. And everything is for sale: mangoes, slivovitz, the complete CD'd Schönberg quartets, durian, bidets, Demal chocolates. Consumerism gone mad is the Tokyo way of life, and the materialist paradise is now – the conclusion of H. G. Wells's *The Shape of Things to Come* has been reached.

Tokyo's façade is, as a result, resolutely contemporary. Though the Japanese like the cozy (the domestic labyrinths), they do not, unlike Londoners, incorporate these into their official attempts at style. Rather, keeping up with the Suzukis, they always put their best economic foot forward.

Hence perhaps another reason for the enormous rate of architectural turnover in Tokyo and, because of a presumed newness, the use of Western models in the buildings built. Bastardizing European style has for over a century been the Japanese way, and Tokyo is studded with early examples: Tokyo Station, a brick edifice that would look perfectly at home in Amsterdam; the Akasaka Detached Palace, which would fit into Vienna without a single comment. Now, with the ratification of the post-modern, influences from East and West swarm in the capital – Babylonian, Baroque and Bel-Air Moderne grouped incongruously together.

Such promiscuous clusterings come naturally to a culture that does not know what the original alluded to and does not care, that uses others' idioms to suit its own meanings, and that is never troubled by having to observe the integrity of any original.

For the pedestrian foreigner, much of Tokyo's frenetic carnival flavour is due to familiar things being used in unfamiliar ways. There is a kind of freedom in finding that Doric columns don't mean banks, nor red roof tiles, Spain. The feeling of being at liberty in Tokyo is occasioned by this 'illiteracy'. There is no telling what anything means.

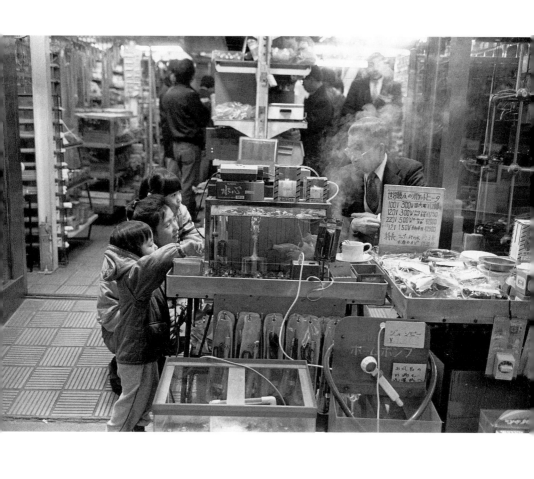

And all of this awash in the great flowing current, the people of Tokyo – a tide, diurnal, nocturnal, always sweeping through this unfinished po-mo-but-trad labyrinth of a place.

In Tokyo, one is reminded of another urban concept. I sometimes wonder why the Japanese went to all the trouble of franchising a Disneyland in the suburbs when the capital itself is in many ways so superior a version. Let us look into some of the resemblances.

Disneyland, and the other lands it has spawned, is based on the happy thought of geographical convenience: all of the interesting localities on earth – African rivers and Swiss mountains, Caribbean islands and American towns – located in one spot. One is seeing, one feels, the world in miniature and, indeed, 'It's a Small World' is the slogan of one of the concessions.

Compare this to Tokyo today. There are hundreds of American fast-food stands, dozens of red-lacquered Chinese restaurants and equal numbers of white-stuccoed Italian ones; there are thousands of boutiques with famous foreign names printed all over them (Gucci, Dior, Yves St-Laurent, Arnold Palmer); there is an imitation Baker Street straight from London; the Museum of Western Art in Ueno has Rodin casts in the front yard; and there is an onion-domed Russian Orthodox cathedral.

In the resulting stew, even the authentically Japanese takes on a pleasantly ersatz flavour. Thus the old Toshogu Shrine in Ueno, a real Edo relic, appears in Tokyo's Disneyland context just as pleasingly synthetic as does the new Japanese modern-style restaurant gotten up almost right as a French bistro. Old and new, Tokugawa remains and new Heisei structures, Tokyo in its entirety resembles Disneyland on a mammoth scale, with an area of nearly 2,500 square kilometres and a working staff of over twelve million.

The reason, of course, is that Japan is the real home of all those concepts which Disneyland has come to exemplify. It is in Japan, after all, that the notion of the microcosm was most fully elaborated – from its beginnings right down to Walkman baby loudspeakers for the ears, wristwatch TV's and the smallest and fastest silicon chip ever.

84

Japan has always displayed a fondness for the geographical microcosm as well, the bringing together of famous places in a single locality. In the far suburbs, there is an attraction called the Tobu World Square where one may view scale models of over a hundred of the world's most famous buildings. The Taj Mahal is next to the Empire State Building, which is next to St Peter's, which is next to the Eiffel Tower, and so on. All are complete down to the smallest visible detail – indeed, they were made by the Toho Eizo Bijutsu, the people who gave us *Godzilla*.

Many small towns in Japan sport a Ginza, a hopeful replica of what was once Tokyo's most famous shopping street; many gardens have a little Mt Fuji, small but climbable, included among the attractions. The classical Japanese garden itself gives an indication of how attractive the microcosmic impulse has been for centuries and how early the Japanese perfected these small, visitable worlds.

Take, for example, the Korakuen in Tokyo, an Edo-period garden. One climbs a small hill which calls itself Mt Lusha (from China) and finds oneself at a replica of the Togetsu Bridge in Kyoto's Arashiyama district, except that the view is not of the river but of a famous lake in Hangzhou. We are back in China again, but not for long. Climb another tiny hill and here is Kyoto once more, the veranda platform of the Kiyomizu Temple, one of the most famous sights of the city.

Some Edo gardens are even more Disneyland-like – Tokyo's Rikugien for example. Here, in one place, arranged somewhat like a miniature golf-course, are most of the 88 agreed-upon canonical sites, all tiny and all with notice-boards explaining the Chinese or Japanese associations.

Such examples are found everywhere. Lest it be thought, however, that these are just examples of big-city, late Edo commercialism, Japan's claim to early Disneyfication might be defended by mentioning Kyoto's elegant Katsura Villa, one of the inspirations for the Bauhaus and the modern style in architecture. Here the garden is a hodge-podge of famous scenic attractions from elsewhere: the Sumiyoshi pine, the Tsutsumi waterfall, the Oigawa river and Ama no Hashidate, the famous wooded spit of land on the other side of Japan.

Kyoto's elegant moss garden, that of Saiho-ji, contains – if one knows how to find them – scenes from ten famous places, reproductions of ten famous things (rocks, etc.), ten poetic references and ten famous pine trees. Even Ryoan-ji's famous 'Zen' rock garden has Disney aspirations. Those rocks are more than just rocks. They are manifestations of the infinite, or they are islands in the ocean; they are a section of the famous Inland Sea, or (a very Disney touch) they are a mother tiger and her frolicking cubs.

The famous twelfth-century Byodo-in is a replica of a Chinese water pavilion, with imitation Chinese swan-boats (phoenixes, actually) being poled and pushed about. And the earliest Kyoto garden (c. 800), the Shinsen-en, is still a replica of Sukhavati, the Western Paradise of the Buddha Amitabha. Those rocks in the pond are the three islands of the blessed – Horai, Hojo and Eishu. And that big rock in the middle is Mt Sumera itself. So, more than a thousand years ago the Japanese had already constructed Space Mountain.

It is thus evident that the Japanese claim to pre-Disney Disney-fication is a strong one. No other country has brought the principle of the microcosm – in ikebana, bonsai, chanoyu and gardens, to mention only its earlier manifestations – to such profuse perfection.

Umberto Eco believes that '. . . real cities redeem, in their context, even what is architectonically ugly.' He holds that '. . . perhaps in New York the Ca' d'Zan of Sarasota [, New York] would be acceptable, just as in Venice, on the Grand Canal, so many sibling-palazzos of the Ca' d'Zan are acceptable.' He has said that '. . . a good urban context and the history it represents teach, with a sense of humour, even kitsch how to live, and thus exorcize it.' Well, maybe. It would be interesting to see how he would explain Japan's rural experiments in the various 'lands' that now spot the landscape.

Most of these lands have foreign themes, perhaps because, as travel writer Cleo Paskal has written,

> . . . today's Japanese tourists don't want to be bothered by the horror, not to mention the expense and trouble, of the real thing.

They want a New York they can visit for a weekend, and a London where everyone speaks Japanese. They want a sanitized Japanese version of the rest of the world – a virtual vacation.

Japan created an early virtual world in Sasebo's Holland Village, an island-built replica of Deshima, that man-made offshore island which was, perforce, home of the first foreigners, and it was here that the Japanese could easily visit a part of their own culture. So popular was this venture that the parent company later opened up Huis Ten Bosch, a land of canals, windmills, tulips and wooden shoes. There are 'European-style' hotels, and those who wish to can buy on-site Dutch houses right in the park and live the life of the Netherlandish burgher without leaving Japan.

There is, naturally, none of the dinge and danger of, say, Amsterdam. The original Dutchmen could view Japan from Deshima as spectacle; now the Japanese can view Holland as spectacle from the comfort and safety of their own land. During its first year, Huis Ten Bosch had nearly four million well-paying customers.

Shortly thereafter, Ashibetsu in Hokkaido – having lost its coal-mining industry – decided to go into the theme-park business. Canada World opened – Japan's largest lavender field, a complete St Edward's Island-like 'Anne of Green Gables' Land and seven resident Canadians quilting, playing the fiddle and chopping wood.

In Niigata's Russian Village, one may, without the difficulty and danger of actually visiting Russia, see Suzdai Cathedral, eat pirozhki, drink borsch and enjoy a folk-song-and-dance troupe and the talents of three performing seals direct from Lake Baikal.

Over in Shingomura in Aomori, you may also visit the last resting-place of Jesus Christ. It was actually his brother, Iskiri, who was crucified, you see. Christ himself escaped to Japan, where he married a Shingomura woman named Yumiko, had three daughters and lived to a happy 106 years of age. His 'descendants' opened this 'Christ's Tomb' tourist attraction.

Then there is Nixe Castle in Noboribestsu, a full-scale replica of the castle and home-town of Hans Christian Andersen; Shuzenji's Britain Land, a slice of seventeenth-century British countryside

87

complete with homes and shops; and Portopialand in Kure, which includes much of Portugal's Costa del Sol in some form or other.

Plus a number of New-Zealand-Valleys in Hiroshima, Yamaguchi and Shikoku, which specialize in sheep shows (an exotic entertainment in non-mutton-eating Japan), and the Tochigi Edomura, Hello Kitty Land, Yomiuri Land, the Yokohama Wild Blue and the Chiba Hawaiian Centre (with wave machine), etc. Here 'kitsch' may be too weak a term. One must turn to Russian and suggest *poshlost* – a word for the preposterously overdone, but overdone with no self-knowlege, no irony.

Though the onlooker at any of these spectacles may be reminded of Dr Johnson's maxim that nothing is more hopeless than a scheme of merriment, the financial success of these various artificial foreign lands within the safe confines of Japan has proven their viability for the Japanese.

After all, places like Canadian World actually let one become a temporary Canadian, whereas if one visited Canada there would be the constant reminder that one was actually a foreigner. Anyway, foreign countries are just too foreign to be readily comprehensible. These 'translated' versions are the best way of understanding them.

Whether enormous Tokyo does or does not lend authenticity to its many virtual attractions (Eco's idea) is perhaps a matter of opinion. What is more certain is the role that these attractions have always played in the excitement, the vitality and, yes, the charm of the place. The frivolities of Edo and the trivia of Tokyo create in large part the sheer pleasure this city purveys.

The first foreign visitors to the country were fond of comparing it to some childlike wonderland and its inhabitants to children. Such adjectives as 'wee' and 'quaint' were used to delineate these qualities; Victor Hugo himself said that Japan was 'a child of the world's old age'.

Assumptions of cultural superiority may account for some of these expressions (as well as rapacious imperial designs: children are easy to subdue), but at the same time, some of the observations are apt. There *is* something childlike, if not childish, about the country.

This is perhaps because many Japanese (like many other peoples) find constant reminders of childhood satisfying and are more open than many other peoples about it. The attractions of childhood are manifest. It is, after all, a time of safety, security, closeness. Various approximations offer a kind of return to this blessed state.

This may account for the fact that adults read comic books, that childish forms of address (*chan*) are used by grown-ups, that bar hostesses are supposed to mother, and that parents go to Disneyland just as frequently as children.

Then too there is the eternal vogue for the cute, the *kawaii*. The police box at Sukiyabashi is done up in *Hansel und Grethel* gingerbread-house fashion, a doll's house with uniformed dolls. The new Minato Ward Office with its toyland colors and doll-house furniture looks like a home for Barbie and Ken. That cute animal, the panda, is so beloved that no-one found it strange when the announcer on NHK, the major government TV station, broke down on announcing the death of one of the beasts at the Ueno zoo.

One might mention, too, the aural atmosphere of the place. Was ever a country, I wonder, so fond of the celesta, the musical box, the upper register of the piano? You wait on the phone and are fed *Für Elise* on the musical box. In the 'bullet train', all announcements are preceded by a phrase on the musical bells. The celesta is heard before NHK announcements, and every station on the circular Yamanote Line in Tokyo has its own musical 'theme', played on the upper reaches of an electronic carillon.

What is this din except the sound of childhood itself – the merry pealing of little bells which we associate with being very young. The cloying sweetness of the celesta, the clinging tones of the musical box – these are the sounds of a childhood captured because it was never lost.

These, and a thousand other things, initially so enchant visitors from abroad and make it difficult for them to take Tokyo seriously. One has too good a time there; one feels so much younger.

Younger in several senses. We are in Tokyo sometimes returned to a stage in our development we had almost forgotten, when we were

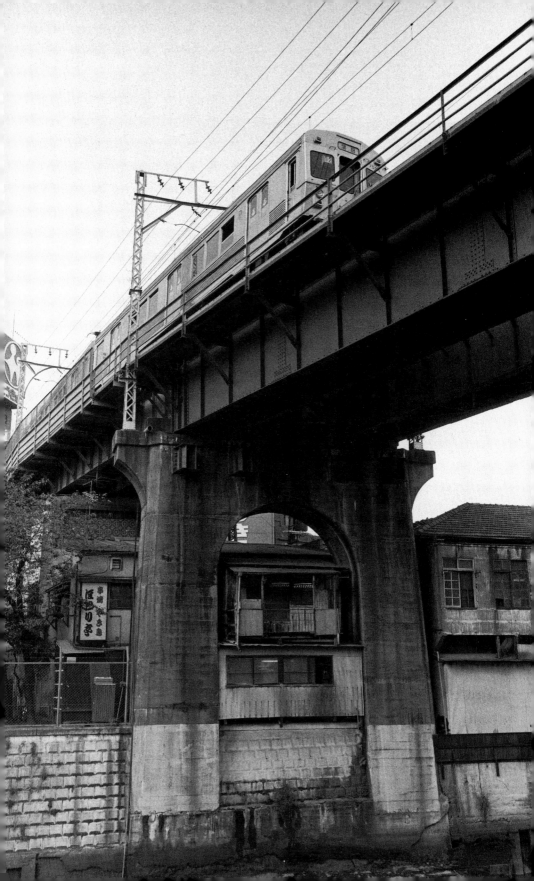

so young that few of the inhibitions we later learned had as yet intruded. Each and every one of us still retains an element of what Freud in his fancy way labelled the polymorphously perverse. Let me explain – but this will take a little time, so perhaps a detour is in order. We will walk around the block while I elucidate.

Edward Saïd has said:

> The more one is able to leave one's cultural home, the more easily is one able to judge it, and the whole world as well, with the spiritual detachment and generosity necessary for true vision. The more easily, too, does one assess oneself and alien cultures with the same combination of intimacy and distance.

Quite so, and the urge to intimacy is indeed tempered by the fact of distance. The foreign visitor will have discovered the difference, one rendered doubly dramatic in that so much that appears Western has been revealed as Western only in appearance: finding in the shoe department something one does not know, looking in the carpenter shop and locating nothing you recognize, eating the Western meal and discovering Japanese viands – for this is the land where even McDonald's sells rice cakes.

The result is a pleasing confusion and a realization that one is, in this country, free of one's own mores and still more or less immune to those of the Japanese. A part of the pleasurable distance is that exceptions are made for the foreigner, the *gaijin*. There is, indeed, an entire Japanese system of exemptions for foreigners.

This results in the ultimate liberty of finding everything *other* than oneself. Walking down the street, one experiences the freedom of being manifestly different. The foreigner was stared at for well over 150 years. Early accounts all mention this, and until the massive influx of foreigners in the 1980s it was still the case. You became used to it, and eventually irritation turned to need. No matter what the people truly thought, you were treated like a star.

Quickly, however, the traveller discovered that Japan insisted that the star keep its distance. Those living in Tokyo were expected to move to Roppongi or Aoyama or Azabu – a move towards High

City ghettoization. There one sometimes found that paradigm of intimacy and distance: the marriage between the foreign man who wanted in and the Japanese woman who wanted out. And yet, though he desired intimacy, Japan was teaching him to keep his distance. (If the foreigner had been yellow or black instead of white – or pink – the lesson would have been harsher and the imposed distance greater.)

Another country, says Alastair Reid, an authority on the subject, is another self. One is regarded as different, and so one becomes different – two people at once. Look at me. I was a native of Ohio who knew only the streets of little Lima, and I am also an expatriate who knows the streets of mighty Tokyo. Consequently, I can compare these places. And since the act of comparison is the act of creation, I am able to learn about both.

I am also free from prejudices of class and caste. I cannot detect them, and no-one attempts to detect them in me since my foreignness is difference enough. I remain in a state of surprise, and this leads to heightened interest and hence perception. Like a child with a puzzle, I am forever putting pieces together and saying: 'Oh'.

Or 'naruhodo', since I have for some time been learning Japanese. And learning a language does indeed create a different person since words determine facts. When I first arrived, I was an intelligence-impaired person since I could not communicate and had, like a child or an animal, to intuit from gestures, from intent, from expression. Language freed me from such elemental means of communication, but it also taught me a lesson I would not otherwise have learned.

While it is humiliating to ideas of self to be reduced to what one says (nothing at all if one does not know Japanese), this condition teaches that there are other avenues than speech. It is like seeing a foreign-language film without titles. I may not learn much about the movie, but I learn a lot about film making.

What I am describing here is what any traveller, expatriate or otherwise, knows, but the degree and the difference depend upon the place and its culture. Japan tends to give foreigners a strong jolt because the space between the distance kept and the intimacy

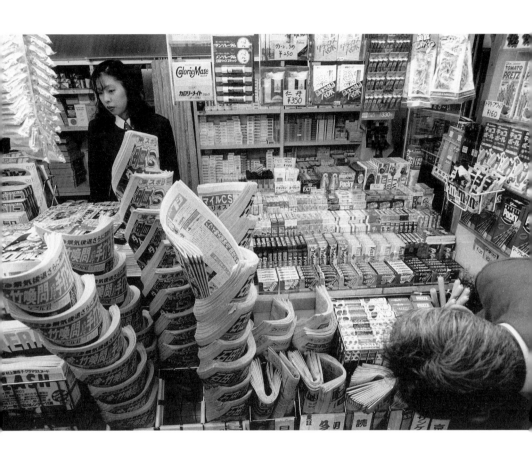

implied is greater than in some other countries. Japan is still openly xenophobic and at the same time has a need for the foreigner that creates an oscillating dialectic – one that affects Japanese re: foreigners almost as much as it affects foreigners re: Japanese.

From the Japanese point of view, the ideal arrangement is for the foreign visitor to come, do his business, and get out. A foreigner who elects to remain is cause for interest and concern. How often it is implied that I would do better to go home. This is not unkind or even inhospitable. People are reacting as they would were they themselves in a foreign land. Many Japanese abroad want to return to Japan, do not travel well, need *miso* soup, etc. They do not think of others behaving differently in like situtations. 'Where are you from?' asks the taxi driver. Told, he asks: 'But you go home often don't you?' Assured that I do, he is mollified.

Given the imposed distance, the apparent intimacy promised by many Japanese becomes doubly attractive. The promise is, I think, not intended. It is occasioned by a real desire to give the guest pleasure, an inability to plainly say no, and a concern for gain.

This means that the foreigner is forever kept up in the air, be it in a business deal or in a love affair. Sometimes, the emotions are identical. I heard a frustrated merger specialist complain about a failed deal with this metaphor: 'There I was, open like a flower . . .'

And the lone person, the person who does not speak the language well, he who never spent his childhood in the culture – precisely this newcomer is most in need of the intimacy that is dangled before him, is always just around the corner.

That this need often takes sexual form is notorious. Travellers almost by definition screw more (or want to screw more) than other people. Partly, it is the freedom ('No-one knows me here'), but mostly it is the need to affirm self on the most basic level, that of emotion. Also, sex is imperialistic since it always implies a top and a bottom, and one of the ways to encompass (and subject) the distant Other is through what is often called the act of love but in this context should probably be called the act of sex.

When this urge meets the seemingly pliable 'native' with her or his 'different mores', the result is a kind of infatuation. It can go

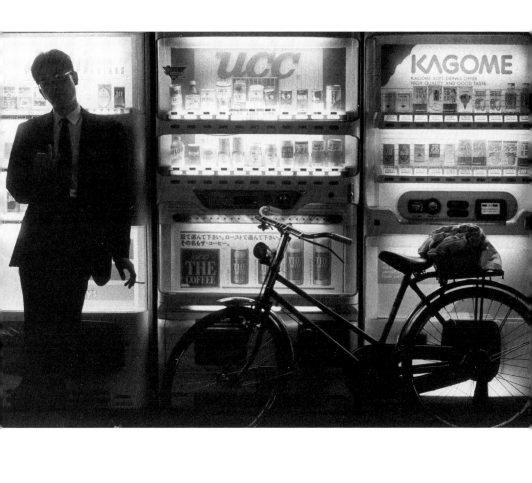

both ways, and often does. But the major consideration is that the Japanese have to 'live' in their country, and foreigners cannot.

Foreigners are, says Allastair Reid, curable romantics. They retain an illusion from childhood that there might be someplace into which they can finally sink to rest: some magic land, some golden age, some significantly other self. Yet the foreigner's own oddness keeps him or her separate from every encounter. Unless one regards this as something fruitful, one cannot be considered cured.

Thank you for your patience; we may now continue. As illustration, let us wend our way to what pass for fleshpots, those districts which cater to the emotional needs not only of Japanese but also of those foreigners who wander into them.

They are numerous, these pleasure quarters, warrens of rejuvenation, where the tableaux of innocence and experience are displayed. The old Yoshiwara beyond Asakasa, the Kabuki-cho district of Shinjuku in the west, and, further out, the new streets of shame in Shin-Okubo.

Here, more a customer than a guest, the interested foreigner searches for the emotional simplicity of what he might have known as a child, if he was fortunate enough.

Here there are parlors for peepers, the *nozoki-beya*, where the innocent voyeur may watch through a window controlled by a 1,000-yen bill. He peers into an almost forgotten world where mama/big sister/auntie takes off her dress and 'does not know she is being looked at'.

There are large closets where you can lock the door and find a significant other on the screen as you share your space with an open box of kleenex and a waste-paper basket. There are other closets with round holes at hip height where amateur enterprise takes over.

For harassed businessmen, there are somewhat more expensive places staffed with girls in nurses' uniforms who fasten executive nappies, wield baby-powder puffs and urge a certain regularity of natural functions.

There are topless and bottomless places with mirrored floors; there are the so-called handkerchief salons where the customer is

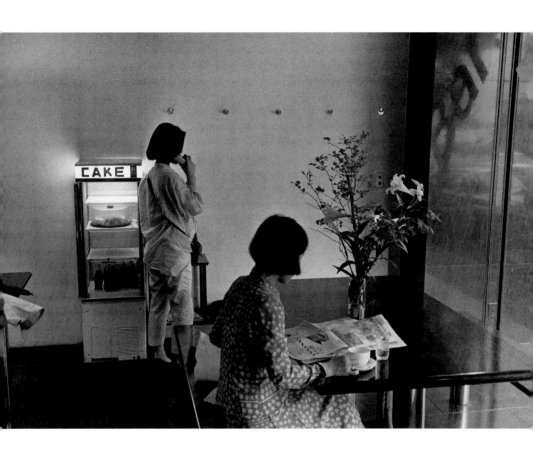

persuaded to pollute his lap, where the contents are caught in a skillfully manipulated linen square, where this square is then folded and tucked into the breast pocket with a single word: 'Souvenir'.

For the adventurous, there are simulated airplanes, train coaches and buses with hired passengers of the opposite sex. For men there are strip joints, and for women there are strip joints; for men there are hostess clubs (women dressed as schoolgirls, as nurses, as hostesses), for women there are host clubs (men all dressed up or dressed in very little).

And for all those many male adults who read lascivious comic books about schoolgirls being tied up, there are establishments where the more wealthy will go to be tied up by women in spike heels. And more, and more, and more.

In this sexual wonderland, the patron, native or foreign, wanders, bemused. The variety, as in the Japanese department store, is staggering; the choice is boggling. But what the foreigner retains from his experience will be the sense of innocence he has newly discovered.

In those underground theatres where girls come on, do their dance and then invite the customer onto the stage with them, one searches in vain for the sordid. Though the act of love more or less inexpertly performed takes place on a revolving stage – professional and amateur united at last – it is not squalid, shameful, soiled, dirty: all the synonyms for 'sordid' that the dictionary could dredge up.

Rather, the spectacle is decorous. There is an appropriateness of behaviour, a kind of propriety, indeed, in so far as it is possible, a kind of formality. Many visitors have noticed this, taking it to be an anomoly. Peter Quennell referred to Japan as a place 'where vice itself is ceremonial'.

Actually, it is as though one has a seat at the revival of the Age of Gold or a season pass to Eden. Consequently, the spectacle is not erotic, though it is palpably sexual. It is not pornographic – for porn you need a bit of guilt, and these entertainments are as innocent as the driven snow. Someone called it asexual kindergarten, and so it is.

But a kindergarten with adult attributes, one of which is the making of money. To be sure, all societies have to an extent discovered in the sex lives of their citizens a powerful incentive to gain, and even left to itself sex tends towards commercialization. How much more useful, then, if this lucrative urge can be channelled to more effective mercantile use.

This idea occurs to all normal businessmen. Discussing Japan's achievements in the field does not indicate that the Japanese phenomenon is in any way unique. Rather, as always, Japan's way is the common one – but more efficient, more effective and much more visible. No-one has shown better than Japan how a natural instinct can be turned into a well-run business.

Japan's sex industry has been estimated as a £25-billion business. This is very large – indeed is almost equivalent to the national defence budget. A quarter of this enormous amount consists of the revenue of the so-called love-hotels. All societies have commercialized sex, but only a few have so marketed the venue, and none to the extent that Japan has.

There are over 35,000 such hotels, 3,000 in Tokyo alone. The rooms range in price from the equivalent of £60 down to half that, for what is called in the parlance of the trade a 'short time'. A longer time, like all night, costs more. Here the price climbs to the height of a certain suite for £1,250, where, to be sure, you are allowed to occupy what is billed as a £5-million 'rococo' bed.

Prices differ for services offered. There are beds that rotate or go up and down; mirror-lined rooms; two-level suites with glass-bottomed bathtubs intended to be viewed from below; 'space-shuttle' beds for simulated take-offs; and, for the ultimate in safe sex, S/M chambers.

In addition, many hotels serve breakfast that includes a popular item, broiled eel, still believed to be an aphrodisiac, and most rooms contain what is called a Romance Box, which holds whiskey, soap and a vibrator.

There is also the latest in TV electronics. Each room has a tube with closed-circuit soft-core porn, and many have self-operated cameras that relay one's own hard-core performance onto the tube

– and, it is said, into the main office as well, where a further profit might then be made.

With such a variety of attractions, it is not surprising that love-hotels rival Disneyland in popularity. The main reason for this is, of course, the lack of other venues. Japanese dwellings are crowded, and couples are correspondingly cramped. Japanese business, in taking advantage of this sociological fact, has as usual given the customer the latest technology. The modern love-hotel is thus different from the older *ryokan*, which has been around for centuries. *Tsurokomi ryokan* – which might be translated as 'drag her (or him) inn' – have all been supplanted by examples on the cutting edge of the trade.

Since it has been ascertained through careful appraisal of the market that it is women who often choose which hotel to go to, the love-hotel's image has been sent up-market. Indeed, the very term *love-hotel* is no longer heard very much. Rather, one speaks of the 'fashion-hotel' or 'leisure-hotel', and while love-hotels had such masculine names as 'Empire', 'Metro' and 'Rex', fashion-hotels have names such as 'Chez Nous', 'Inn Lively' and the popular 'Once More'.

In addition, the better leisure-hotels are arranged so that from parking the car to paying the bill, the couple is never directly viewed. Entry is electronically controlled as is payment, privacy is assured, and no-one at all sees the happy pair – unless, of course, they unwisely elect to commemorate their performance on tape.

Second among money-making sexual outlets is an outstanding example of adaptation in the world of Japanese business, the 'adult' bath-house, something quite different from the neighbourhood bath-house. Though the Japanese businessman is often accused of rigidity (not opening up markets, not assuring a level playing-field), we can see just the opposite here: how the sex bath-house has accommodated itself to changing times.

The problem originated back in 1984, when a Turkish diplomat complained that such baths – which had become the principal purveyor of the commodity after the passing of the apparently in-effective 1958 anti-prostitution laws – were called Turkish. Indeed, *toruko* had become the most common term of reference.

Always sensitive to the feelings of others, the Tokyo Special Bath-houses Association met and determined that the 110 affiliated bath-houses were amenable and would change their designation.

But to what? In order to determine this, a democratic method was devised. The public, appealed to, responded with numerous suggestions – some 2,000 postcards were received. Among the contenders were 'Romanburo', 'Colt' (that is, 'Koruto', an anagram of 'Toruko') and 'Rabuyu' (a felicitous combination of 'love bath' and 'love you'). The winner, hands down, was 'Sopurando', or Soapland.

Note the simplicity of the construction: a suggestion of cleanliness – soap – and a proposal of pleasure – Disneyland. This construction – so typical of Japanese accommodation when it is called upon – was an instant success. Prices rose to match the level of dignity of the new title, and more efficient money-making methods were employed. Calling out an attendant by name now cost a bit more; there appeared an unexplained but dignified *atobarai*, unspecified charges when you checked out; and the categories of service – special service, double service, extra special service and full course (the latter being what we might call making love) – were more strictly insisted upon. But there were perks as well – for example, the new 'fashion massage', a service that the patron had formerly been forced to practise upon himself.

At the same time, in addition to such main-line money-makers, there were speciality venues. There progress varied, but there were some examples of enterprise. Take, for example, the *nozoki-beya* already mentioned. At first, there was merely the upper window; then another appeared, also operated by a 1,000-yen note, somewhat below waist level.

These had been popular for years, voyeurism having been heavily marketed in movies and *manga* alike. But the market had stabilized itself and even shown signs of falling off. In particular, the charms of that lower window were found to be limited.

As though in response, an innovation – from one of the enthusiastic workers herself – recently sprang into view. A customer put in his customary note, and, instead of the window, the door opened.

There, before the surprised patron, stood the girl herself. 'But you are supposed to be inside,' he is quoted as having said. 'It's just too much trouble,' she said and pulled him to her.

Thus do institutions change their shapes, and voyeurism's loss is business's gain. Actually, the woman pulled her patron into the much more lucrative mainstream. It is indicative that the innovator was female, because it has become increasingly evident that the female market is clamouring for attention. With the largest disposable income now in the handbags of unmarried women, the Japanese sex business is being transformed from a females-for-males service industry into an even more level playing-field.

There were earlier signs of this: the proliferating and highly lucrative host clubs, for one. Now, however, there are – for example – a growing number of male strip shows for women. The strippers are, at present, all foreign, white or black, but it seems just a matter of time before the potential for part-time work among Japanese males is realized as well.

Not all, however, has been growth and profit, and it would not do to paint too rosy a picture within these speciality markets. Though the various S/M establishments in the country have shown a healthy gain, other markets have not. Particularly disappointing has been that sober venue so misleadingly called the 'gay' scene.

Here it is a matter of mercantile concern that little development is occurring. Rising profit remains basic to the health of any drinking establishment, yet most homosexual bars have, scandalously, not raised their prices in the last five years. Drinks, unbelievably in modern Japan, still cost a mere £3, and one is allowed, unaccountably, to nurse this single drink for most of an evening. A note of hope, however, is that lesbian bars are among the most expensive in the city, and snacks are served whether wanted or not – a sure sign that sane business sense is prevailing.

In general, however, the gay scene exhibits only economic degeneracy. There are no racks of theme T-shirts, no guided tours, no Gayland concept at all. If ever an area needed development, it is this one.

Leaving this depressing subject, it is a pleasure to turn to the most innovative and successful of the recent forays into the sex market, one that has indeed been milked of its full potential. This is the previously mentioned video box.

Like all great business concepts, the idea is simplicity itself: a large room in which stand a number of large boxes. The customer enters one of them and locks the door; this activates a TV, into which he inserts his 1,000-yen note; the soft-porn film begins; the only other accoutrements in the box are an open box of tissues and a waste-paper basket.

The beauty of the idea becomes apparent. Japanese business know-how has harnessed one of nature's most universal urges and has persuaded the patron to pay for a pleasure hitherto wastefully free. I cannot think of another nation that has had the vision, the imagination to take such successful advantage of such an enormous market.

There are, in addition, new means of marketing, offering insight into the enterprising world of sex business in Japan. One of the most successful means has been the vending machine. Not only do these purvey alchohol, tobacco, soft drinks and hot lunches; they now do their bit to satisfy an increasingly open demand for sexual satisfaction.

There is, for example, in this age of hopefully safe sex, the lucra-trive condom industry. Though for the up-market buyer there are now rubber boutiques such as the extremely successful Condomania in that heartland of the young, Harajuku, there is no doubt that the greater number of prophylactics are sold by privacy-insuring coin-operated machines.

Now, in a bold new step, these same machines sell porn videos. Patrons need no longer make the sometimes embarrassing visit to their corner shop. They can in perfect anonymity purchase porn for as little as £12 per title. To be sure, this is soft pornography, and enter-prising businessmen remain unable to open the market up further.

To obtain what is known as 'the real stuff', the corner shop must still be visited a number of times until mutual trust between owner and patron is built up to the point where the area under the shelf is displayed.

The difficulty is that, since Japan has no censorship laws as such, there is a problem when it comes to defining what is obscene and what is not. For a time, a useful line was drawn at pubic hair. Anything with it was obscene, anything without it was not. This led to a number of anomolies, shaved models among them, but they at least defined the field.

Magazines and books entering the country were routinely cleaned of hirsute details by squads of housewives working part-time and equipped with special equipment that scraped the areas in question free of any image whatsoever.

Inside the country, however, it is apparent that the pubic-hair line is not holding. Recent major magazines have breached it. There has been some retaliation – the printer of the Japanese edition of Madonna's coffee-table book *Sex* was fined – but before long, enterprising Japanese publishers were following this bold lead. As always, a healthy business sense prevailed and it became apparent that an enormous market existed. With money to be made on all fronts, there are now many fewer police-led crackdowns on pornography.

There are also new ways of making new productions available. One of these is the marketing of used 'schoolgirl' underwear in vending machines. The mercantile effectiveness of this is unquestioned: bought for as little as £1 the unit, such underwear is sold for as much as £30. In just a month, an enterprising trio of three men made over £90,000. Obviously, there was a public out there. Equally, there was an abundant source. Newly rich schoolgirls working hard to use their underwear playfully referred to their new employment as *H-baito, baito* coming from *arubeit*, a common loan-word for part-time work, *H* coming from the romanization of *hentai*, which means 'perversion'.

To be sure, there is some criticism of such sales practices. The Education Ministry took an interest and finally decided that the panty entrepreneurs might have broken the Antique Dealings Act.

These, then, are some examples of the highly successful commercialization of a commodity in Japan – one which, despite setbacks, has attained heights that might well render the foreign businessman envious. Enterprise, imagination, application and sheer single-mindedness have turned an instinct into a industry in Japan, have carved an empire from an urge.

Having completed our stroll and looked into some of the results of a child-like innocence (lack of guilt) coupled with an adult-like experience (interest in profit), we may continue our walk along the byways of Tokyo and begin to notice something more about what we are seeing and about the way we are seeing it.

'The tendency of the Japanese to view nature in its parts rather than as a whole,' writes Hasegawa Nyosekan, 'is fully apparent in the arrangement of Japanese cities.' They have, he says, no atmosphere; they show few cultural characteristics; wherever one goes, the confusion of the newly built-up rules: 'The result is as though a box of toys has been upset – the product of the individual whims of a lot of feebly Western-style architects.' The Ginza, for example, spills its toys most extravagantly. Each building stands isolated, its eyes closed to its surroundings. These are merely lined up as at an exhibition, proud in their individuality, without a care for where they are: 'No overall atmosphere can emerge and chaos reigns.'

Japan has, indeed, long cultivated a kind of partial vision, and this is seen particularly in the sights of Tokyo. One is advised to admire the famous old shrine and, since one is not Japanese, one also includes the gas station next door, the TV aerial in back and the supermarket truck in front, and is consequently disturbed.

It is doubtful that a native sees all of this, because he or she is gifted with partial vision, the ability to ignore that which would encroach upon the famous shrine, the single ancient pine or the once wide vista of the sea. The West does not encourage vision this selective, but in Tokyo it is almost a necessity.

In a place this crowded, there is no such thing as a 'pure' view. Consequently, impurities must become invisible. One sees this principle at work in many other areas. At the better hot-spring *onsen* hotels, for example, you are literally invisible to the help until you are washed and dressed and desire to be seen. It is then and only then that you are addressed. Carparks, acres of bikes, oil refineries, strip-mining are ignored in the same way.

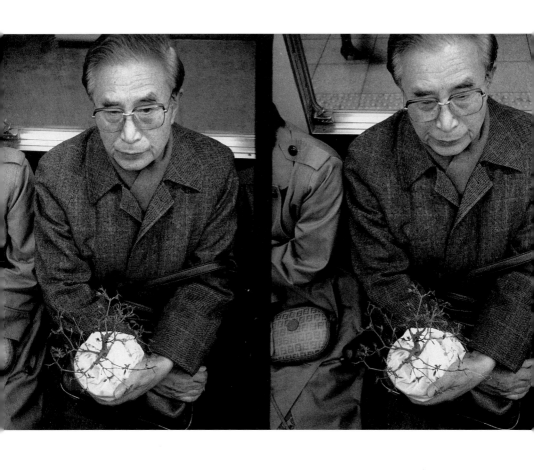

When one looks at the view, one looks *at* it and only it. This is a way of viewing for which the camera is famous. It can edit out what it does not want. One can frame or zoom, and the undesirable is gone as though it never existed. Since they share this gift, most Japanese are notoriously fond of the camera. As they ought to be – cameras approximate their own learned vision.

This vision is presentational. It makes a selection among availabilities and proffers it. In this sense all views are partial, and indeed there are few full-scale, in-your-face frontal views of anything. Except for several shrines and temples, a couple of banks or company headquarters, there is no feeling of frontality at all.

This is a contrast to the West, where frontality is itself a kind of presentation. Buildings are designed to be viewed full on, and this primary stance is deemed important. Everything is shown. But this means a viewing space – a square or plaza in front of the edifice, often two or three times as wide as the viewed object is high. This is impossible in crowded Japan.

The intentions attributed to the viewed object must take another form. One of the reasons that the Sukiyabashi police inhabit a gingerbread house is that the display is intended to stress the benign quality of the national police force.

Most countries experience some kind of presentational imperative: each country has its own political ends, its own ritualistic needs and, consequently, its own near-theatrical codifications. In any comparison among these, I feel that Japan would rank high, that as a culture it experiences a strong need for ritual and hence exhibits a wide range of near-theatrical manifestations.

Among the various origin myths, I think only the Japanese one offers a paradigm for theatre. The circumstances are related in that ancient 'history' the *Kojiki*. In a fit of pique, Amaterasu Omikami retired to her cave. Since she was the Great Divinity Illuminating Heaven (a translation of her name), she left the world in darkness. She was lured out again by the merrymaking – dances and the like – feigned by other deiities. Curious, she peered out from her shelter (the first *nozoki-beya*) and was drawn forth to illuminate her world once again. It was a presentation, a performance, that was the salvation of the land. The theatrical paradigm was in place from the very first.

Japan is certainly not alone in creating such myths as this, but it is, I think, very nearly the only culture to so plainly label its solar myth as a performance. The goddess is fooled, the merrymaking is feigned – it is all false – and this is approved.

While it is not unusual for the legends of other cultures to include some kind of performance (Judas kissing Jesus is a dumb-show for the centurions), it is highly unusual that this be approved – given the blessing, as it were, of both Shinto church and Yamato state. I think it can be said that Japan early on expressed a theatrical urge and has continued to manifest this in much of its culture.

A familiar example is traditional Japanese architecture. Though much influenced by that of Korea and China, this way of making a building is – as many have noted – rather like making a stage. The reference is to the traditional Japanese house, which many earlier observers saw as a performing area. It was raised off the ground, like a stage, it had no fourth wall (indeed, it had no walls at all), and its interior divisions could, like stage sets, be moved about at will.

Admittedly, one cannot make too much of this because such structures share a good deal with domestic architecture elsewhere, but inside this theatrical house is a smaller theatre that might be unique to Japan.

This is the *tokonoma*, an alcove in the main room of the traditional house that serves as a place of presentation – nowadays mainly of a flower arrangement or a scroll, or both in some kind of artful juxtaposition.

To be sure, here too there are Eastern antecedents, and the West has something similar in its furniture of display, the what-not, the china closet and so on. In Japan, however, the theatrical analogy is much stronger. Not only are there featured players – the scroll, the flower arrangment, sometimes the valuable vase as well – but there are frequent changes of bill as the seasons pass.

The *tokonoma* as stage has thus built into it the spatial and temporal considerations that limit and define the theatre itself. It might thus be used as an indication of a presentational urge in Japan.

Another indication might be the way in which domestic nature is presented. The Japanese garden is well known, indeed nearly notorious, for being a contrived spectacle. This stone is moved over a metre, and that bamboo stand is moved back two. The pebbles or sand are brought in at great expense, and the view of the distant mountain is purloined and called borrowed scenery. This is the 'natural garden'.

One might argue that European and Middle Eastern gardens are even more constructed, with their balanced symmetry and geometrical intentions. And so they are, but the inventors and admirers of these gardens never called them natural, which is just what the Japanese assume theirs to be.

Nature has been presented. Tidied up, stylized, it has been made – as the old garden manuals have it – to express nature better than nature itself does. It is presumed that the integrity of any original does not exist. As in any dramatic presentation, the only integrity is that of performance.

Not only does nature in the form of the Japanese garden become spectacle – as in, for example, the garden at Ryoan-ji – it also becomes the theatrical experience itself – as in the Edo garden, where as you stroll about vistas are disclosed, scenes hidden and then revealed in a manner most reminiscent of the stage.

Even more theatrical is the art of ikebana. Here the stage is prepared (the *tokohoma* or its modern equivalent), the presentation has rules (never mind that these 'living flowers' are now dead), and – as in naturalist theatre – the aim is to make the real more real than reality itself.

Or, to put it in the best possible light, as Count Herman Keyserling observed:

As to Japan, the understanding of nature of its inhabitants is so inordinately great that they have subjugated their surroundings aesthetically; in the same way as a patch of color can determine and change the meaning of a picture, the Japanese by deliberately inserting his particular existence into surrounding nature has transferred the keynote of the latter completely into himself.

Let us continue our stroll through the city. Descending from the modest citadel of the old castle, we proceed through the circular byways down to the mercantile maze. We will continue on to the Low City, then off to the High City and out to the suburbs, onto the plain of Musashi on which Tokyo lies. Let us also consider what we are doing.

One walks for various reasons. Often it is merely to get somewhere. The street is seen as a stretch connecting one place with another. Sometimes, however, it is seen as itself. One is going no place in particular. We look at the street and not the destination.

This makes walking in Marrakesh different from walking in, say, Chicago. And walking in Tokyo is different from either. Streets here have their ostensible and mundane uses, but they also have something more. They are areas of display, and you are the audience. There is so much to look at.

This makes us a spectator. One is, in Walter Benjamin's felicitous phrase, 'botanizing on the asphalt'. Strolling slowly, looking simply for the pleasure of it, one becomes what Baudelaire called a *flâneur*, an observer who has no reason for observing except the pleasure of observation. Benjamin further observed that this gaze of Baudelaire's *flâneur* 'bestows a conciliatory gleam over the growing destitution of men in the great city'.

Which is how he explained one's becoming an *homme des foules*, a man of the crowds. But one can view the crowded street without becoming too concerned about destitution. It is possible to look without making moral judgements of this sort. Particularly if the city is – unlike, say, nineteenth-century Paris – safe.

Baudelaire may well have asked '. . .what are the dangers of the forest and prairie compared with the daily shocks and conflicts of civlization,' but we could not ask this of Tokyo. One may have observed, as did J. M. Richards (quoted by Mark Girouard), that the Japanese, 'having totally tamed their countryside, deliberately kept their jungle in the cities', but this does not explain the inordinate

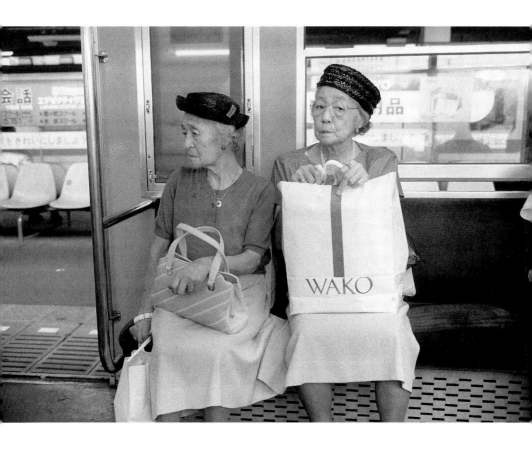

safety. Any woman (any man as well) may walk anywhere at any hour in perfect safety.

Yet, with the difference of being safe, certain sections of Tokyo do indeed still somehow contain signs of the past. Girouard has said that Tokyo is sometimes still like Paris a century ago: 'If one wants to get any feeling of what Montmartre was like in the 1890s, one is more likely to do so in Asakusa or the Yoshiwara than in the sleazy streets of Montmartre today.'

All cities have their Shitamachi, an old downtown, a section earlier, older, a place where one may find what remains of history. New York has its below-Canal-Street, London has its East End. Neither of these cities, however, makes as much of its downtown as does Tokyo. To the Japanese, particularly the native Tokyoite, the capital used to be divided. There was the Low City and then there was the rest.

The rest, the High City, the Yamanote, is by far the larger part of Tokyo, but it is taken for granted. The Shitamachi was made much of, spoken of as something special, its people unique. Someone born in New York's Fulton Street or along London's South Bank was just another city dweller, but someone born in the Low City was something else.

He was (if the product of three generations in that locality) a real *Edokko*, a child of Edo. He embodied and displayed a number of distinctive qualities and thought of himself as being open, generous, hot-tempered, quick-witted, inquisitive, generous, quick to offense and quick to forgive. He found himself spontaneous and impulsive, traits one does not associate with modern Japanese.

So different did he find himself from other Tokyoites – and naturally from those in other cities, especially those money-mongers in Osaka – that he coined a number of wise sayings, one of the most striking of which was: 'Always spend the money you make in the same day.'

If the *Edokko* resembled another downtowner, it was not the Cockney (a parallel often stressed), but the sponanteous and impulsive Elizabethan. Indeed, there may have been a time when all

112

Japanese were like this – before the beginning of the Tokugawa reign. One would like to think so, because even now there are places which have managed to escape the full weight of this repressive government and consequently share something of an Elizabethan quality: the people of Kagoshima, of Kochi, of Choshi, resemble those of Edo's Low City.

The reason the people of old Asakusa, the riverside part of Shitamachi, escaped was not distance, as in the cases of Kyushu's Kagoshima and Shikoku's Kochi, but the peculiarity of their territory and its history.

Originally, Asakusa and beyond were a plain of flowering grasses – hence the name. The Lady Nijo visited the temple there in 1289: 'To get there I had to pass through vast fields so densely covered with bush clover, reed, and pampas grass that no other plants were able to grow in them. The height of the grasses was such that a man on horseback could pass through unseen.'

Despite its beauty, however, the place enjoyed a singularly bad reputation. An ogre lived in her cottage on the moor, goes one story, and travellers disappeared with noticeable regularity. It was not only dangerous, it was the ends of the earth. In the Noh play *Sumidagawa*, the distraught mother seeks her missing child all the way to Mukojima ('the island over there'), an area now just across the bridge from the Asakusa branch of the Matsuzakaya Department Store. Also – an important consideration – the land lay to the north-east of the castle, a direction considered by geomancers to be the least fortunate. Consequently, the area was neglected.

One further consideration is that although the Sumida River ran through the Low City, it was never to Tokyo as the Arno was to Florence or the Seine to Paris. The city did not grow around the river; indeed, the castle was some distance from it. Edo was a city created by fiat and by rulers, not by nature and by common folk trying to make a living and seeking cheap water transportation.

For all these reasons, the land on which the Low City stood was not highly valued. It was turned over to the merchants, the purveyors, the poorer townspeople and the priests.

There were a number of the latter, and their many temples

served to keep the dreaded north-eastern influence from the castle and its tenants. The main Asakusa temple was ancient (tracing its beginnings back to the seventh century), and a new building, the Kinryu-san (Temple of the Golden Dragon), was completed in the middle of the seventeenth century by Iemitsu, Ieyasu's successor. In 1682, however (on 18 March say the temple records), some fishermen found in their nets a small statue of the Buddhist diety Kannon – the so-called Goddess of Mercy.

Such a miraculous find so near a large and prosperous temple resulted in a popular name for the place. The temple began to be called Kannon-sama, and, though its official name has been changed several times (it is now Senso-ji), it still is. The building was destroyed (along with the entire area) in the Second World War, but the postwar concrete edifice remembers the original dragon in a large ceiling mural, and the faithful still come to pray to Kannon-sama.

Come in their thousands, even now, which is the reason that an entire city originally grew up around the temple, one that was encouraged by the government since it could banish there those entertainments thought disruptive in Edo proper. So it was to Asakusa that restaurants, drinking stalls, entertainment parlours, theatres and the licensed quarter went.

The latter area, north of present-day Asakusa, was the famous Yoshiwara, one of the most celebrated red-light districts of Asia. Flourishing until the anti-prostitution law of 1958 was passed, it consisted of house upon house, woman upon woman – something for everyone and someone for everything. Before the Second World War, it still had great painted palaces, like those seen under the sea by Urashimataro, illuminated picture-windows filled with women. Until the turn of the century, it had hosted the great procession of courtesans. The *oiran*, teetering on high-toothed sandals, one white hand resting lightly on the shoulder of the servant shielding her with an enormous bamboo umbrella, her white face a mask, her kimono alive with colour, proceeded slowly through the open street, a rare being escaped as if from some celestial aviary.

Edo Castle had regulated human appetite to a geographical

position, and there, for a time, it left it. Though there were many investigations and reforms, Asakusa and its environs were not usually subject to the repressions inflicted upon the rest of the city. Among the reasons for this were the facts that such a pressure-valve was necessary and that increasingly the financial affairs of the city were falling into the hands of merchants, themselves fond of such ostentatious pleasures as the latest fashions, the world of the Kabuki, and the fabulous licensed quarter.

It was they who fed the great pleasure machines of Yoshiwara/ Asakusa which we now know from the prints and pictures, novels and plays that the place produced. Saikaku's loving ladies review lives of amorous adventure; the grand courtesan Yatsuhashi walks the boards; Sukeroku (samurai in disguise) comes up from the provinces and sees life lived as it ought to be. The actors and wrestlers of Sharaku, the courtesans of Utamaro look at us out of woodcut prints and show us what it was like back then.

To view the moon from a brothel veranda, surrounded by courtesans who knew their classics: this was the world of the *ukiyo*, the floating world of transient pleasure – the maple leaf exceptional only in the deepening hue that showed its nearing end, the cherry blossom meaningful only as it fell.

One pursued one's lesser ends – making love, making money. One did not fight with life; one drifted elegantly with its current, living for the moment, carried along by one cared not what, like (a description by an *ukiyo* poet) 'a gourd floating downstream'.

This at least was the ideal, one much at odds with the stern Confucian castle. In Yoshiwara, one celebrated each new fashion (an odd colour worn by an actor, a singular way of tying one's sash) and cultivated an attitude known as *iki*, which combined what we would now call being 'with it' and an assumed insouciance that refused to assign any importance to the very qualities being celebrated. Within the castle, one did nothing of the sort.

The elegant diversions of Yoshiwara were reflected in the more plebian pleasures of Asakusa itself, the vast grounds around the Kannon Temple. But this pleasure ground did not really develop its own identity until the collapse of the Tokugawa regime, the removal of the Emperor to Edo, and the designation of Tokyo as capital of Japan.

The great Kannon Temple brought in the crowds, but it was the great pleasure city, Asakusa, that entertained them. Even foreigners knew this. A. B. Mitford listed some of the attractions in the mid-nineteenth-century, including wild beasts and performing monkeys, automata, conjurers, acrobats and jesters. The 1891 Chamberlain/Mason guidebook, as reported by Seidensticker, found that

> the grounds of Asakusa are the quaintest and liveliest place in Tokyo . . . performing monkeys, cheap photographers, street artists, jugglers, wrestlers, life-sized figures in clay, vendors of toys and lollipops of every sort, and, circulating amidst all these cheap attractions, a seething crowd of busy holiday-makers.

There were other kinds of liveliness as well. An early foreign observer, W. E. Griffes, noted that near the temple were ranged the archery galleries,

> presided over by pretty black-eyed Dianas, in paint, powder and shining coiffures. They bring you tea, smile, talk nonsense, and giggle . . . and then ask you leading and very personal questions without blushing . . . Full grown able-bodied men can find amusement for hours at such play.

And later on, in back of the stalls as well, for these black-eyed Dianas were in it for the money.

With its attractions of sensationalism and sexuality, Asakusa prospered. One of Tanizaki's characters – protagonist of a story, 'The Secret', translated by Anthony Chambers – indicated the protean joys of the Asakusa of 1911:

> Changing my costume every night so as not to be noticed, I plunged into the crowd in Asakusa Park . . . I enjoyed using a false beard, a mole, or a birthmark to alter my features. But one night, at a second-hand clothing shop . . . I saw a woman's lined kimono with a delicate check pattern against a blue ground, and was seized with a desire to try it on.

Later, in an unfinished novel, *The Mermaid*, Tanizaki tells what Asakusa was like in 1918. Its attractions were (in Ken Ito's translation)

> plays of the old style, operettas, plays in the new style, comedies, movies – movies from the West and Japanese productions, Douglas Fairbanks and Onoe Matsunosuke – acrobats balancing on balls, bareback riders, *naniwa bushi* singers, girl *gidayu* chanters, the merry-go-round, the Hanayashiki Amusement Park, the Twelve-Storey Tower, shooting galleries, whores, Japanese restaurants, Chinese restaurants and Western restaurants – the Rairaiken, won ton, chow mein, oysters over rice, horsemeat, snapping turtles, eels, and the Cafe Paulista.

There was also the Asakusa Opera, where opera was actually sung in the beginning. One early attraction was *Rigoletto*, and 'La donna é mobile' became a local hit although, no tenor being available, the Duke was sung by a soprano. Shortly thereafter, however, the attractions became more varied. Here Tanizaki's hero discovered

> caricatures of Charlie Chaplin, and living reproductions of such stars as Pearl White, Ruth Roland, Doris Kenyon, Billie Burke, and Dustin Farnum. The reproductions were, of course, crude knock-offs . . . but they charmed the audience precisely because they were crude.

The Asakusa Opera also meant flesh on view, the firm thighs of the chorus line. In a story published in 1946, 'The Decoration', Kafu remembers (in Seidensticker's translation) what it was like:

> Backstage was given over to clutter, such a clutter that you wondered how anything more could possibly be added. An indescribable disorder . . . what first caught the eye, however, was not the violent jumble of colors, or even the faces of the girls as they sprawled about on the floor and then sat up again. It was the powerful flesh of the arms and legs . . . it called to mind the earthen hallway of a florist's shop, where a litter of torn-off petals and withering leaves is left unswept and trampled into shapelessness.

Crudity became an Asakusa commodity. The hero of Tanizaki's unfinished novel is both put off and attracted by it. He confides that he is drawn to Asakusa because, finding Tokyo ugly, he wants to experience this ugliness in its purest state. He suggests that '... since seeking beauty in this city of Tokyo is useless, can it not be said that the most agreeable place to live is Asakusa, where ugliness bares its essential form?'

This crude and ugly but vibrant and sexy Asakusa was shortly destroyed. The 1923 Kanto Earthquake demolished it, as it demolished much of Tokyo and Yokohama. Among the more famed disasters was the collapse of the Asakusa Twelve-Storey Tower (the Ryounkaku, or Cloud-Surpassing Pavilion), a brick structure that had become synonymous with the area. Also gone was the old neighbourhood structure of the place. That sense of community, raffish but real, which had appealed to so many.

As a pleasure city, an entertainment capital, one of the great night towns of the world, however, reconstruction began at once. And now, symbolizing the new Asakusa, there was the Subway Tower Building, with its observation platform. Kawabata Yasunari said of it that it was in the Osaka style, all the floors except the top one being eating places. This influence of the mercantile Kansai on what was left of old Edo was commonly lamented. 'Why, it's gotten just like Osaka' commented a character in one Kawabata story.

Actually, it was like no place else on earth. In commenting on Kawabata's later novel, *The Crimson Band of Asakusa*, in 1939, Kataoka Yoshikaza described the new Asakusa as that 'human market' where 'everything conceivable is flung out in its raw state' and 'all human desires are given full rein.' In the new Asakusa,

> the pleasure resort of the Edo period, the vestiges of the crude, semi-enlightened curiosity of the Meiji era, and the over-ripeness of the present era of capitalist corruption are thrown together in a forever disordered state. Or organized in a manner peculiarly like the place itself. Eroticism and frivolity and speed and comic-strip humor; the bare legs of dancing girls and jazzy reviews; kiss-dances, foreign girls, ground-cherries and popular

songs; the movie, the circus, the fake, dilapidated aquarium and insectarium. Here the girls bob their hair and 'bobbed-hair' so-and-so, wearing a red dress, plays the piano, deep in a narrow backstreet lane, with her knees exposed. Her rendezvous notes are scribbled on the back of the Goddess Kannon's written oracles . . .

Like Montmartre in the 1890s, like New York's Times Square in the 1940s, the place was license itself. Soeta Azembo (again in Seidensticker's translation) described it in heightened terms: 'Asakusa of the myriads flings everything forth in the raw. All manner of desire dances there naked. All classes and all races mix into one great flow, limitless, bottomless, not distinguishing day from night. Asakusa is alive.'

Among all these varied attractions, one of the most popular was the cinema, a form of entertainment early associated with Asakusa since the first Tokyo movie house, the Denkikan, had opened there in 1903. Here one could see the wonders of the West; after 1932, one could even hear Marlene Dietrich and Gary Cooper talk to each other in *Morocco*.

In his 1937 *A Strange Tale from East of the River*, Nagai Kafu wrote that (as translated by Seidensticker)

> young and old delight in moving pictures and make them the subject of daily conversation, and even a person like me sometimes feels inclined to wonder what the conversation might be about. I always make it a special point, therefore, to look at billboards when I pass moving-picture houses. One can tell by the billboards, without seeing the pictures themselves, what the general plots are, and what delights people so.

By 1930, Kawabata noted, Asakusa had fourteen movie houses. He also stated that it had even more legitimate theatres. In addition, his survey continues, there were half a dozen vaudeville (*yose*) halls and one Kabuki theatre, as well as the largest number of pawn-shops in the city, and also the most beggars: in the summer of that year, some 800 were said to be living in Asakusa Park, though the author did not trust this official estimate and maintained that there were far more.

It was the stage that Kawabata preferred, in particular the Asakusa Review, which opened in 1929 at the Kasino Fori (Casino Folies). He described the review as comprised of 'eroticism and nonsense and speed, and humor in the vein of the topical cartoon, the jazz song, legs'. *Eroguro* was the spirit of the age. This combination of the first syllables of *erotic* and *grotesque* typified that combination of the sexy and the absurd. There were, on the one hand, the firm-thighed chorines and, on the other (since Meiji times, it was said), the lady who smoked through her navel.

Kawabata made the Folies famous in his novel, though their leading comedian, Enoken, claimed that their popularity was merely based on the false rumour that on Fridays the chorus girls dropped their panties. The novelist also gave us our only real record of what the place was like. *The Crimson Band of Asakusa* showed it at its most Asakusa-like: hedonistic, grasping, frivolous, frenetic and filled with flesh.

Kawabata described Asakusa in its pre-war prime. Soon the place began its decline. Exotic bloom that it was in increasingly illiberal Japan, it began to fade. By 1938, the novelist Takami Jun (translated here by Seidensticker), wrote that

> the famous old places of Asakusa had been abandoned . . . the birthplace of the Asakusa review was in advanced neglect, the subject of weird stories. Late at night, it was said, you could hear the sound of tap dancing on the roof. It has since been torn down and so those who loved the Casino Folies have lost all trace of their dream.

Yet Asakusa continued on with remarkable vitality and to the end managed to retain something of its earlier charm. Jun wrote in 1939 that Asakusa still had a 'peculiar kind of warmth'. It was like 'a jazz record blaring forth in an alien tongue', but '. . . it becomes all shyness and awkwardness like a girl with an old-fashioned coiffeur and an advanced bathing suit.'

In a city that saw its pleasures and freedoms curtailed as Japan left behind the liberties of the '20s and '30s and marched towards the wartime austerities of the '40s, Asakusa remained to indicate that there was more to life than serving one's country. It might have been mercantile, but it was also acceptingly human. Kawabata noted in *The Crimson Band of Asakusa* that a popular song of the day got it right: 'Asakusa, the pulse of Tokyo / Asakusa markets humanity.'

The military takeover of the '40s subdued the Asakusa spirit even more, however. Seidensticker shows us Nagai Kafu one cold night in 1944 recording the closing of the Opera House, his favourite venue: 'As I passed the lane of shops . . . on my way to the subway, I found myself weeping again . . . I have been witness to it all, Tokyo going to ruins.'

It went completely to ruins in 1945. In the American incendiary raids of 9 and 10 March, between 70,000 and 80,000 people were killed and some two-fifths of the city were destroyed – including Asakusa. The Kannon Temple was hit at 1:30 a.m. and was consumed in two hours.

After the conclusion of the Pacific War, the Allied Occupation authorities gave much of the land to the Kannon Temple which, having no money, sold it. Thus Asakusa Park with its famous pond disappeared. The area behind the temple was turned into a parking lot for tourist buses; another portion went to a motion-picture company, which built a theatre and an amusement hall.

That post-war innovation, the strip show, became visible from 1948 – more flesh than ever before seen, with variations as well: the bath strip, the tightrope strip, etc. But all this activity was illusory. Tokyo was moving West, Shinjuku was the new night town, and Asakusa was forgotten. By 1966, one newspaper headlined: 'Deserted Place: Thy Name is Asakusa'.

Since Asakusa was no longer alive, it could be taxidermized – that is, gentrified. Land prices being what they are, it was seen as a smart business move to make a kind of Asakusa-land out of Asakusa. Cheaply made, jerry-built, hopefully post-modern structures were called Denkikan and Rokko after genuine Asakusa landmarks.

But the crowds were gone. The only people who go regularly to Asakusa now are those who go to play the horses at the enormous Racing Centre and those who are too poor to go elsewhere. When night falls, there is no-one there. The hopefully posh restaurants have closed for good, most of the major theatres are no longer standing, and Asakusa is much like any other depressed neighbourhood. The ogre is long dead, the house on the moor long razed, the traveller goes unafraid, but the flowering grasses have vanished. And yet . . . Tokyo always, if only for a day, remembers:

May 21, 1978. To the Sanja Matsuri in Asakusa, that annual spring festival which for a day returns Tokyo its rural ancestry. Bands of men (and nowadays women) carry the mighty *omikoshi* float on their shoulders, bouncing the happy god aloft in his portable shrine, wearing festival clothes from earlier times, pressed against each other, shoulders and cheeks against the wood and the gilt, feet moving together as though each had become part of a centipede, lurching together, chanting, shouting, each caught, finally, gratefully, in the grip of something larger.

And for every person participating, one thousand who had come to see. By two in the afternoon the press was such that one could not move. *Nakama doshi* – just us together – in every street, all held in the sway of the god in darkness, swaying in his shrine. An exciting, exhausting sight.

I gaze at the tattooed men – floats with the fully tattooed standing aloft, swaying; decorated men naked but for a *fundoshi* loincloth, straining and heaving under the shrine; older men with belts and kimonos open, just a glimpse of rare old tattooing, leading the holy procession through the streets. A small, handsome, middle-aged man, strong legs, a slight paunch, cloth-strip around loins, cloth strip around head. Up the left arm swims a carp, down the right arm glides a carp, just that, and a scattering of cherry blossoms. Perspiring tattoos – Kannon as though weeping, Kintaro as though sweaty with exertions, Fudo glistening in his painted fire as though covered with fresh blood.

Foreigners are always encouraged at this matsuri. Japanese

are here so fully enmeshed with each other that they can drop the national xenophobia. They become Elizabethan again, filled with gusto and cheer. I always feel like an early emissary – perhaps fifteenth century, probably Portuguese. It is all very friendly as well. At the Sanya Festival is the only time I have ever been touched, handled by the Japanese – by unknown Japanese, at any rate. A comradely hand, a glimpse of history – more, a view of the Japanese as they might have been before the Tokugawa cookie-cutter descended. A haze of fellow-feeling and good-cheer. Up to a point. Promising conversations are always cut short by the magic call of the shrine and its god and all those waiting compatriots.

Ueno, a twenty-minute walk (now a five-minute subway ride) from Asakusa, is also Low City, but it is quite different. Even the temple bells of the two places are traditionally separate. In an old haiku, such a bell is heard and the poet asks: Ueno? Asakusa?

But the poet knows. The places are really not at all alike. The novelist Saito Ryoku (as quoted by Edward Seidensticker) wrote: 'Ueno is for the eyes, a park with a view; Asakusa is for the mouth, a park for eating and drinking . . . Ueno is silent, mute; Asakusa chatters on and on.'

One of the reasons for Ueno's relative dignity was the proximity of the rulers. Many were buried there eventually (one can still visit the tombs of the shoguns near Uguisudani Station), and the rest kept paying visits. Among the other reasons was the mighty Kanei-ji temple compound, built under Hidetata, the second shogun, in 1625.

It was one of the sights of Edo, an enormous collection of buildings placed in the geomantically correct north-east position. One was called the Toeizan Temple in graceful reference to the temples atop Kyoto's Hieizan. It was decorated by Jingoro, the woodworker who did the famous sleeping cat at the Nikko Tokugawa mausoleum. In just twenty days, he completed two great pillars, both holding dragons, one ascending, one descending. No sooner were they finished than the priests found them dripping wet early one morning. They were so life-like that they had been bathing at the large pond beneath the temple.

This manufactured legend gives an indication of Ueno's original character. In a city with little history, legend could provide explanations. Also, historical structures could be approximated. One such (unlike the original Kanei-ji) is still standing. This is the smaller copy of the Kyoto Kiyomizu-dera, which is here called the Kiyomizu Kannon-do and which overlooks the Shinobazu Pond.

Below, in the middle of the pond, is the home of another female deity. This is the Benten-do, a post-war copy of the original octagonal building dedicated to a rather florid goddess, perhaps Hindu and one of the seven quasi-Shinto deities who made their way to the shores of Japan. No goddess of mercy, Benten is musical (she plays the lute) and much given to lubricity. Next to her templed island is a small rocky islet where, fittingly, sits one of the last phallic stones from old Edo. From the front, the image is a priest with a cowl over his head. From the back, it isn't.

Above the pond, past the torii and up the steps is one of the few Edo-period structures left, the Toshogu Shrine, now somewhat neglected but still speaking of the past. It is here that Jingoro's dragons are now to be found. All the rest of the mighty complex went up in flames during the battles of 1868. Here the last of the Tokugawa loyalists engaged the imperial forces and were routed, but not before setting fire to magnificent Kanei-ji.

There are several temple gates that still show their bullet holes. Standing in the plaza at the entrance to what is now Ueno Park is a statue of one of the heroes of the fracas, Saigo Takamori, himself a rebel against the government he had fought to install. Because of the circumstances of his death (ritual suicide), he is not dressed in full uniform as bronze statues usually are. Instead, he wears a simple, short robe, and the casual nature of his attire is emphasized by the dog on a leash which accompanies him. His widow, upon seeing this statue, is said to have exclaimed: 'But he never dressed like that!'

Just ten years after the battle, things had so changed that Mr and Mrs Ulysses S. Grant could walk about the park that the place had become, plant a few trees (still standing), and perch on the little porch of the Kiyomizu-do and admire the view. And 50 years later, things had changed so much more that Nagai Kafu, wandering through Ueno, could look about him and observe that even though the city more and more resembled some English-American colony, still, if one could imagine chancing upon some corner where a shade of past glory remained, this corner would be at Ueno, among these abandoned tombs.

Something of the official (as contrasted to Asakusa's unofficial) remains in Ueno: most of Tokyo's museums are located there, as well as a number of libraries, several concert-hall complexes and the zoo. The park, Tokyo's largest, aerates the city much as Central Park aerates New York. Though not so heavily wooded, Ueno contains more trees than any place else in the city except for the forest still standing around the Meiji Shrine right in the middle of the High City itself. Everything is well maintained, filled with decent city strollers. Though the place is also a commercial centre (which Asakusa no longer is) and has its raffish side, it remains respectable. Originally pretentious and official, it has now become civic. Though a part of the Low City, it is already looking towards the High.

A 45-minute walk (some eleven minutes by subway) leaves the Low City behind with the New approaching as one reaches the Ginza – not only that wide avenue we have been walking along since Ueno but also the blocks of streets on either side. There are over 50 of these within the eight blocks east of the avenue, and an almost equal number to the west.

The Ginza proper, the avenue, is only eight blocks long, from Kyobashi to Shimbashi; bridges at either end once marked these termini. The street continues, to be sure, but its name changes. From Kyobashi up to Ueno, it is called Chuo-dori.

It is also one of the earlier straight streets, a planned thorough-fare. Though the area was originally a nondescript strip of land crowded between daimyo residences and the homes of the Tsukiji townspeople, the particularly disastrous fire in 1872 (3,000 houses destroyed though only three people killed) provided the opportunity for a rare bit of city planning.

At the same time, it was felt that Tokyo needed an up-to-date neighbourhood, a place where the New, which was flooding the country, could be properly viewed by both natives and visitors. The fire-break that was the Ginza was transformed into an imitation Western town, with two-storey brick houses, the first sidewalks and gaslights.

Though nothing remains of this strange creation, it lent the Ginza its reputation as the home of the new, the residence of fashion, a reputation it maintained for many years. By the 1930s, the Ginza had become self-consciously stylish. It was written about as 'the outdoor Peacock Alley' and 'the Mecca of Tokyo night life'. One social critic wrote that '. . . to be children of the Ginza is to be truly modern.'

The children were the *moga* and the *mobo* – portmanteau terms for 'modern girl' and 'modern boy', the former with spit-curl and cloche, the latter with plus-fours and cap. Here too came all those others to whom a stroll on the Ginza was an hour in the modern world.

This occupation, strolling on the Ginza, was described by a term one still hears: *ginbura*, the first syllable coming from Ginza, the latter two from the word for sauntering. The street became one of Tokyo's first (and last) promenades. By 8:00 in the evening, wrote one commentator, '. . . the *ginbura* is in full swing . . . even well-known actors and actresses are seen shopping and promenading along the street.'

Well-known foreigners as well. Charlie Chaplin and Paulette Goddard (and her chaperone mother) were to be seen, as well as Jean Cocteau (with Marcel Khill), who later wrote that '. . . la contraste entre les buildings and leurs kimono est si vif qu'on est tenté de me mettre leurs mines et leurs fourrires sous des ombrelles plates . . .'

One took refreshments at the Columbin, a *pâtisserie française* which had a ceiling painted by Leonard Fujita; one bought paper and incense at the Kyukyodo (still there) and cakes at Kimuriya (also still there) and the fashionable new wristwatches at the

Hattori Building (now Wako), the corner building with the clock on top which remains the symbol of the Ginza. There was also the famous Café Plantan, which survived until the 1945 air-raids; it was there that the term *ginbura* was apparently coined and Tanizaki famously said that to use such a term was sure proof that one came from the provinces. Originally, said Matsuyama Shozo, the painter who ran the Plantan, the word referred only to those idlers and good-for-nothings who hung around the Ginza. These early *flâneurs*, however, were soon supplanted by more respectable individuals who came to stroll and shop.

Shopping became a major industry along the Ginza. The big department stories (Mitsukoshi, Matsuya, Shirokiya, Takashimaya, Matsuzakaya) all established themselves along its length. In addition, there were a number of speciality shops, including that of Mikimoto, the 'Pearl King'. This emphasis on money was fitting because the land upon which the Ginza was built had been the district (*za*) where silver (*gin*) had been minted.

Money was spent in other ways as well. The waitresses in the cafés of the Ginza became notorious. Nagai Kafu, an expert in such matters, said that they were like the unlicensed prostitutes so abundant in Western cities. They were called *suito garu* (sweet girls) – both they and the *garu boi* (*boi* meant 'waiter') became one of the attractions of the Ginza cafés.

One anonymous account, written in English and intended for foreign eyes, described a Ginza rendezvous:

Most of the visitors take beer and sake; whiskey and cognac are the liquors for young swells, and those mixed with soda water are often welcomed . . . At one corner you find a young lady and an old gentleman sitting by a small round table between them. The lady is in her Japanese dress a la mode and the man is in European clothes. On the table is an emptied bottle of soda water and a cup full of coffee stands before the lady, and the man, who keeps a glass of beer in his hand and is very red in his face, is secretly appeasing her. All right, you are quite right. Then, what you want for me to do – eh? . . . He then claps his hands (this is the Japanese habit of call maid-servant) and the couple hurries for Shimbashi Station. What are they? The drunkard and the belle! The big old rat has been caught by a small mild cat!

The Ginza with its chains of light, its kilometres of neon, its strolling throngs, its pleasure-bent crowds, was destroyed on one warm March night in 1945 when American B-29's dropped their tons of fire-bombs on the city. Ginza slowly emerged from the conflagration, but it never recovered. Though the famous street stalls reappeared (now selling the detritus of war rather than the latest foreign fashions), the Hattori Building became the 8th Army PX, and the Matsuya Department Store became the Allied Commissary. Up the street, the Imperial Hotel was taken over by American staff officers, and down the street the bombed-out ruins of the Kabuki-za remained.

That which was not destroyed by war was now set upon by peace. Money slowly left the Ginza and travelled further west. Such movement is, of course, a part of the history of the city. To travel as we have done from the Low City into the High is to move in time as well as space. Asakusa, Ueno, Ginza, Shinjuku are temporal strata. They were, in turn, the financial centres of Tokyo, the place to which the crowds came, in which the most money was spent.

The Ginza is now a shopping street like any other, and it closes, like any other, when it gets dark. No more kilometres of neon. The lavish bars and cabarets of the post-war era are now all shut – bankrupt or otherwise out of business. No-one does the *ginbura* anymore, and the *moga, mobo, suito garu* and *boi garu* have all metamorphosed. They are now to be found in Roppongi, that crossing once near the barracks and now near the discotheques, or in that shopping paradise for the young, Harajuku, or in the last and largest of Tokyo's night cities – Shinjuku.

Regarding the Japanese propensity for pleasure, Lafcadio Hearn wrote in an 1895 letter to Basil Hall Chamberlin: 'Here, remember the people *really* eat lotuses; they form a common article of the diet.'

He was referring to the national talent for enjoyment and

indulgence – after the rigours of duty, the pleasures of frivolity. The Edo official tired after hours of duty went to relax in the pleasure-town to the north. The Tokyo office worker exhausted after hours of work goes to lose himself in the night city to the west: Shinjuku.

Some sixteen minutes by subway from the Ginza (and more than an hour by foot, did anyone ever attempt it), Shinjuku is a common business district by day and an extraordinary pleasure warren by night. The west side now contains the Tokyo Town Hall and other assorted skyscrapers, and Shinjuku Station is said to be the busiest in the world, but the place is much more famous for its east side. Here are located the various night-towns that make up this extraordinary nocturnal city.

Unlike Asakusa, which grew naturally around a popular temple, Shinjuku was, like Tokyo itself, created by decree. In 1698, it was felt that a new post station should be built along the Koshu Kaido, the road that entered from the west, since both horses and riders needed to rest. Shinjuku (the name means 'New Lodgings') was the result. Another was that, like most post stations, it became a brothel district. It was consequently closed and then, in 1772, opened again on provision that appropriate taxes would be paid on whatever businesses thrived there.

In just a few decades, there were over 50 inns inhabited by pros-titutes known as 'serving girls'. These had nothing like the fame of the Yoshiwara girls and were called, Paul Waley tells us, 'flowers in the horse dung'. In the Great Kanto Earthquake, Yoshiwara burnt down and Shinjuku didn't. It prospered.

Something of what it must have been like can still be seen in the section known as the Golden Gai (also known as Shomben Nakacho, which might be inadequately rendered as 'inside pissing quarters'), a small, crammed warren of questionable bars and disreputable-looking drinking stalls with rooms upstairs. Though developers have been at work for years, the owners are hardy and have not as yet agreed to being evicted. Walking these narrow lanes with the smell of sake and toasted squid in the air, amid the calls of the women and the lighted lanterns of their shops, it is possible to imagine the Shinjuku of long ago.

Elsewhere, too, the ancient air of licensed pleasure perseveres. In East Shinjuku are whole buildings devoted to indulgence. Like stacked plates, these edifices contain restaurants and bars on every floor, a vertical version of the horizontal warren. Each is slightly different from the other, for Tokyo nightlife tries to seem as individual as Tokyo architecture, and whole sections are given over to specialities.

The area around Shinjuku Two-Chome, for example, was originally one of the two red-light districts (the other was around Hanazono Shrine, merging into the Golden Gai) where 'girls' stood in front of lighted doorways and beckoned. After 1958 and the new law, they offered cameras or sketch pads and pencils, announcing that they were models. Business did not thrive. For one thing, the metropolitan police cracked down in anticipation of the 1964 Olympics. For another, the homosexual community — not the kind of customers the resident girls had in mind – decided to flock there, and there it still roosts.

Like everywhere else, Japan practises double standards – this is as true of sexual mores as it is of trade procedures. There is the rigid official standard, that of the government, of politicians and of the press. Then there is the personal standard of the average person, which is relaxed indeed.

The visiting foreigner, once he has come to understand this, perceives Japan as one of the most sexually permissive places on earth. But if he runs up against the law or the press, he will suddenly find himself in the Victorian age. Everything is forbidden. Urinating on the street, a common offense, is covered by the public-decency laws. Couples petting in public parks are liable under the anti-obscenity laws. These laws are rarely enforced, but the wise visitor should steer clear of official Japan while doing what he wants.

This is what the wise Japanese does. He pays lip-service to the laws, is a strong believer in public morality, then goes out for an evening in Shinjuku and does anything he feels like doing. It is not a question of hypocrisy; it is a question of expediency. He will cluck his tongue disapprovingly at the rise in vice and will then go and willingly surrender himself to the ministrations of a local employee.

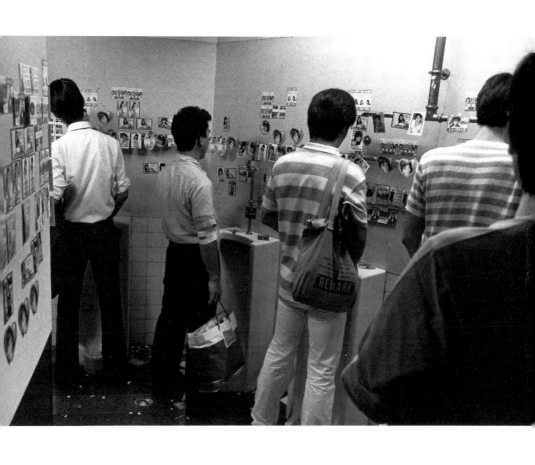

Kabuki-cho, a section of Shinjuku to the west, is the usual destination. Its name has nothing to do with the national drama (at one point, politicians decided to rebuild the Kabuki-za there; they didn't, but the name stuck) other than that it concerns itself with the permissive indulgence that the old Edo kept alive on its stage.

Shinjuku, more than offering opportunity, specializes in offering the air of opportunity. Shinjuku at night seems an enormous palace of a thousand delights, all of them presumably available. Walking the brilliant alleys, smiled at by countless young women as they stand in their doorways or on corners ('Just come in and have a beer'), surrounded by thousands of other pleasure-seekers, one feels that right here, just around the corner, is the experience, the person, the face, that one has always needed to make one whole. Love, one knows, is near.

It isn't – at least, not any nearer than it ever is. But Shinjuku maintains the feeling that it is, a wonderfully wrought emotional illusion. One can wander happily all night long. Comes the dawn and one is philosophical. Oh, it's there all right; one just didn't happen to find it, a wrong turning somewhere. There is always tomorrow night.

Like all really good night-towns, Shinjuku offers a continued and unredeemed promise. One of the reasons is its prodigal display; another is the good will of those out to make money. This makes Shinjuku seems so electric, so vital, so alive that it does not seem to be a part of Japan.

Yet it is. It is just that it is different from the official version. Indeed, it is, in its way, a microcosm of Tokyo itself. Big, sprawling, forever metamorphosing, packaging all the advantages of over-crowding with all the charms of free enterprise. Noisy, forever under construction, Shinjuku is not (despite its share of rip-off joints) hostile or (money-grubbing though it is) cynical. It is massive, crammed, bewildering, but it is also warm and filled with the wonderful innocence of just being alive. If old Edo – Tokyo's legacy – is to be found anywhere, it is in Kabuki-cho at 11:00 on a Friday night.

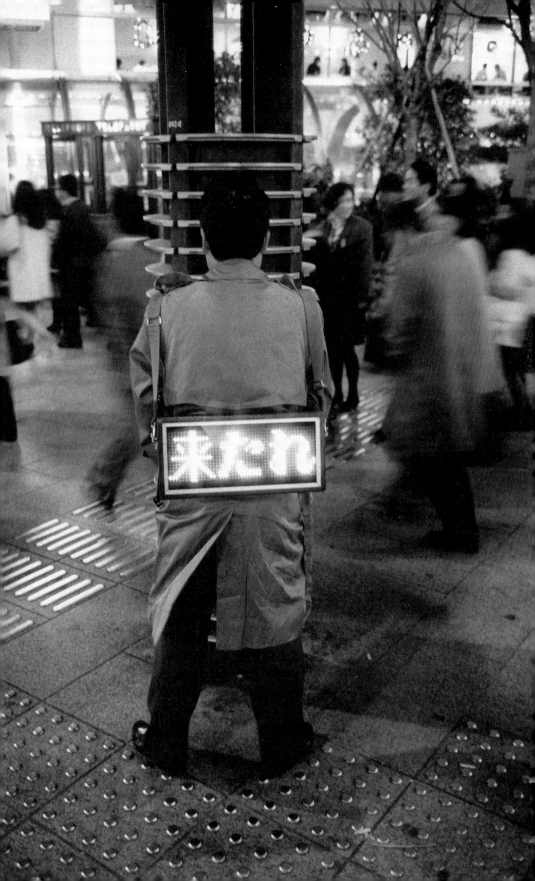

Tokyo, this changing city – the more one gazes, the more one realizes how singular it is. Lafcadio Hearn recognized this one January day in 1895 when he wrote a letter to Sentaro Nishida in which he noted: 'There is no Japan like Tokyo.'

Indeed, and now in a double sense, since Tokyo has spread itself across the land. Tokyo language has smothered the dialects, Tokyo cuisine has driven out provincial specialities, Tokyo fashion has pushed aside regional dress. If there is no Japan like Tokyo, it is because everything is the capital and in this sense there are no more provinces.

A city, a country, in flux. We are surprised because ours are apparently not, at least not in so large, noticeable, definite a manner. Looking at Tokyo, one is reminded of the Buddist condition *shogyo mujo*. All is transient, impermanent; nothing is fixed, all is in motion – life is illusory. Tokyo is in this sense a Buddhist capital, a mandala illustrating *mujo*, impermanence itself.

A people, the Japanese, inured to this are in a way like the early Christians. Both expected human suffering and were used to it. All of life's injustices were accepted precisely because in these religions – being Buddhist, being Christian, being Japanese – this life was a vale of tears. It still is.

People who believe this are tractable. They are trained to put up with a good deal, encouraged to believe that this is their lot. The control of the Church in the West, the control of the State (the Shogunate) in Japan, was the result.

This faith in the future renders the present fleeting, transient, impermanent. Human beings and all their works are subject to time and its work. Even space itself is mutable. It is not to be defined as something contained within walls. It is fluid and in constant transformation.

Space is not, consequently, empty. Though the West has long defined it as such, as something to be filled, both China and Japan still think it something other. Both believe that the essense of all things is this undefined quality, which the Chinese call *chi* and the Japanese, *ki*.

Lao Tzu, the Chinese philosopher, explained this nothingness with the example of a vase. Though it was made of clay, the essence was in the emptiness within. Thus the enclosed, the defined, was 'full' of essence. He said nothing of the emptiness outside, however. It is only the controlled, used, appreciated, enclosed space that is not empty. It becomes something that is to be separated from the emptiness outside. There is a difference between these two kinds of space.

The Japanese do not need to fill a container (a vase, a picture, a room, a narrative, a floral arrangement, a tea ceremony) – it may be left as it is (what we call empty) because it is enclosed (by its structure, its architecture, its perimeter, its purpose) and is hence already full.

One still sees extensions everywhere: the dichotomy between outside and inside; the private garden, the public street; the nameless others outside, the named insiders – the *nakama*, just us, our gang. But for how long, I wonder.

Yoshinobu Ashihara, a contemporary architect, thinks not for long. As industrialization advances, he says, the attachments that grow out of a sense of community fade. Residential areas fill up with huge company apartment complexes where corporate hierarchy reaches out even to the home life of employees, 'where people must dwell in concrete boxes, situated in a townscape they can have no voice or role in creating'.

The sense of community becomes artificial, attached to corporation or government. The ties of married life, of family, the natural *nakama*, are loosening. Younger people choose the anonymity and impersonality of the big city. They choose the blind gaze of organization rather than the stares of community.

Henry James, speaking of the modern city, said that it was 'crowned not only with no history but no possiblity of time for history, and consecrated by no uses save the commercial at any cost'. He had the 'skyscrapers' of New York (*c.* 1910) in mind, but he might have been speaking of Tokyo nearing the year 2000.

Tokyo grows; the expected population U-turn has never occurred. As I write, the newspaper informs me that the city's permanent population has hit 11,824,617. (I am among the 16,822 Americans living here . . . there are only 6,654 British.)

And since the city was designed (in that it was designed at all) for a small space, this means a geometrical increase in specialized demand. Water, gas, sewage, garbage – all are much more complicated now and demand a more complicated system of administration.

Tokyo grows not only sidewards, across the river, over the plains, but up and down as well. Demand overrides tradition. Japan as prone to earthquakes has been forgotten because it would cost too much money to remember.

Already there are gaps in the infrastructure. The homeless are not housed because the family always looked after its own but now it doesn't. The young are not trained because mother and father both work and expect the school to do it, but the school has no provisions for doing so.

Standards are declining; this shows in small ways. Even a decade ago, people did not eat on the street; now, in the days of 'finger-lickin' good', everyone does. Even five years ago, a person standing on a street corner, sitting on the subway or in a concert hall, shouting, mobile phone in hand, would have attracted censure. Not now. There is now no resistance to the *shinhatsubai*. Convenience is ultimately stronger than tradition.

I have often wondered where the old *shinhatsubai* go. They disappear, all these expensive new products. I suppose they become garbage. This is now a matter of some civic concern, though not enough for anyone to do anything about it.

As Tokyo spreads further and further across the Kanto plain, it must cast its waste wider. The city manages to toss out some 20,000 tons a day of what it no longer wants – this includes not only sewage and other organic garbage but bicycles and refrigerators, air conditioners and automobiles.

Again I am reminded of one of Calvino's cities – this time, Leonia. Here is a city that refashions itself every day, and '. . . you can measure its opulence not by what is manufactured but what is thrown out to make room for the new. A fortress of indestructible leftovers surrounds Leonia, dominating it on every side, like a chain of mountains.' In Tokyo, the amount of garbage doubles every ten years. The landfills are almost full.

We are now in the rapidly filling suburbs to the west. Looking back, we can see the towers of Shinjuku reddening in the reflected setting sun. Beyond lies the distant Tokyo through which we have travelled. Invisible, somewhere there in the east, is the modest citadel – the pine groves, the empty centre.

Over the years, I have looked out upon this metamorphosing city. The roofs change. Grey-tiled, slanted, curved – this meant something traditional underneath: wood, sliding doors, *tatami* mats. Now it also means expense: wood is dear, sliding doors don't hold the heat. So the roofs change. The houses are concrete blocks, apartments, no roofs at all. Ferro-concrete is cheap and holds the heat. Electricity bills go down in such boxes.

The view has changed. The grey-tiled roofs made a natural pattern like bark on a tree. Now there are fewer trees as well. They are too expensive. Nature is a luxury when it occupies land so precious that a plot the size of my desk costs more than I will ever have in the bank. A garden or a grove is no longer to be afforded – which is why such ground now becomes an apartment, or a convenience store, or a parking lot. Somewhere for people to gather.

People – how many of them, how many more than there were. The landscape is crammed with them. No kimono, of course. People stopped buying them years ago. This lack of sales meant higher unit prices. So few are now sold, so few are now made, that the price is almost beyond the means of all. The ones you see are often rented – for weddings, funerals, those rituals where tradition meaninglessly maintains itself.

My view has become a crammed mosaic, a die-cut vista, a thousand people to one tree. Need one be a romantic to regret this? I think not. One is allowed nostalgia in face of the inevitable, when one remembers a time when people could afford to live less crowded lives, could see a tree as a part of themselves. Something is taking its place, to be sure, but at the same time something is crowding it out.

Yet something also remains.

August 4, 1978. In the evening I go to the summer festival, the annual *ueki-ichi* at Shinobazu in Ueno. The wide, shallow pond, dark with leaves, filled with large pink lotuses, each tightly closed into a big bud. Night, the shore outlined with red and blue lanterns proclaiming the name of their donor – Kirin Beer.

Under them the stalls: all kinds of bonsai – one perfect minature red maple selling for £600; rocks, big and little; fish stalls with many kinds of goldfish swimming, specially bred, enormous heads like bull-dogs, or long fins like the tails of the sacred roosters; the insect stalls with little cages holding a bell-bug, or a katydid, larger cages with struggling stag-beetles in them; shaved-ice sellers, glazed squid stands, makers of spun sugar, crystallized cakes of brown sugar, or fruit in ice on sticks; the minnow game with hooks that bend and paper nets that dissolve; fried soba; glass animals; quilted beasts; fireworks sellers.

Japan in the summer is always more Japanese and never more so than at this fair. Families in summer yukata, clacking along on *geta*, gang boys hawking in cummerbunds and shorts; old gentlemen shuffling about in *suteteko* and underwear tops, carrying fans; girls back from the bath with wet hair sleeked back, towels in hands. This is what Japan once looked like. Summer brings it back again. And old attitudes as well. A sudden interest in nature, here in the bowels of the city. Exclamations at the size of the lotus buds. And a much slower tempo. No one striding, everyone strolling. And with it the old politeness. People standing to one side for each other. Nor are they self-conscious in their 'native' dress. This is because these few summer weeks are still the proper time for it. They get out the yukata every year. Usually there is dancing as well but last night was too early. The tower is ready, and the drums are there, but the dancing circle is empty. People wander around it but no-one even attempts to dance. It is not yet the time nor the place.

I go look at the single phallic stone left, on its little wooded island next to the temple of Benten. Then I eat fried soba at a little restaurant put together of straw and wood and rope on the edge of the lake and watch the budded lotus, pink and heavy. They will open at dawn.

And I remember Kafu. In the early part of the century, he was regretting the passing of the latter part of the century before. And in the middle of this century, he was complaining, remembering the early part of the century. Fifty years from now, this time about which I am complaining will probably have become someone else's golden age.

Sources

Abe Kobo, 'The Dead Girl's Song' (Shinda Museum ga Utatta) (Tokyo, 1954)

Alcock, Rutherford, *The Capital of the Tycoon* (London, 1863; reprint New York, 1969)

Anon., *The Hidden Order: Tokyo through the Twentieth Century* (Tokyo, 1989)

——, 'Kanto, Koshin Slammed by Heavy Snow – Again', *Daily Yomiuri*, 16 January 1998

——, 'Population of Tokyo', *Japan Times*, 15 February 1998

——, 'Tokyo's Vulnerability Exposed', *Japan Times*, 16 January 1998

Aristotle, *The Politics* (London, 1953)

Ashihara Yoshinobu, *The Aesthetic Townscape* (Cambridge, 1983)

Barthes, Roland, *Empire of Signs* (Paris, 1970; New York, 1982)

Benjamin, Walter, *Charles Baudelaire* (Berlin, 1969; London, 1973)

——, *Moscow Diary* (Cambridge, 1986)

Bestor, Theodore, *Neighborhood Tokyo* (Stanford, 1989)

Borges, Jorge Luis, 'The Immortal', in *Labyrinths* (New York, 1962)

Bradley, Simon, and Nikolaus Pevsner, *The City of London* (London, 1977)

Calvino, Italo, *Invisible Cities* (1972; New York, 1974)

Chesterton, G. K., *What I Saw in America* (London, 1923)

Curzon, George, *Tales of Travel* (London, 1923)

Drohojowska, Hunter, 'The View from the South', *California* (June 1989)

Eco, Umberto, *Travels in Hyper-Reality* (London, 1986)

Edo/Tokyo Museum Foundation, *Guide to Edo/Tokyo Museum* (Tokyo, 1995)

Engels, Friedrich, *The Condition of the Working Class in England* (London, 1848)

Enright, D. J., *The World of Dew* (London, 1955)

Fussell, Paul, *Abroad: British Literary Traveling between the Wars* (Oxford, 1980)

Girouard, Mark, *Cities and People* (New Haven, 1985)

Graves, William, 'Tokyo', *National Geographic* (November 1986)

Griffes, W. E., *The Mikado's Empire* (New York, 1876; reprint 1976)

Guest, Harry, ed., *Traveller's Literary Companion: Japan* (Brighton, 1994)

Hasegawa Nyosekan, *The Japanese Character* (Tokyo, 1966)

Ito, Ken, *Visions of Desire: Tanizaki's Fictional Worlds* (Stanford, 1991)

James, Henry, *Essays on London and Elsewhere* (London, 1893)

Jinnai Hidenobu, *Tokyo: A Spatial Anthropology* (Berkeley, 1995)

Kami Ryusuke, *Tokyo: Sights and Insights* (Tokyo, 1992)

Karan, P., and Kristan Stapleton, eds, *The Japanese City* (Lexington, KY, 1997)

Kataoka Yoshikazu, '*Asakusa Kurenaidan*', in *Introduction to Contemporary Japanese Literature*, ed. Kokusai Bunka Shinkokai (Tokyo, 1939)

Kawabata Yasunari, *The Crimson Band of Asakusa* (Asakusa Kurenaidan) (1927), trans. Joanne Bernardi (unpub.)

Krupat, Edward, *People in Cities* (Cambridge, 1986)

Lee O-Young, *The Compact Culture* (Tokyo, 1984)

Lees, Andrew, *Cities Perceived* (Manchester, 1986)

Lowell, Percival, *The Soul of the Far East* (New York, 1888)

Maki Fumihiko, ed., *Mie Gakure Suru Toshi* (Glimpses of a Hidden City) (Tokyo, 1980)

Michaux, Henri, *Un Barbare en Asie* (Paris, 1933)

Mitford, A. B., *Tales of Old Japan* (1871; reprint Tokyo, 1966)

Mumford, Lewis, *The City in History* (London, 1961)

Nagai Kafu, 'The Decoration' (Kudan) (1946), trans. Edward Seidensticker (Stanford, 1965)

——, *During the Rains* (Tsuyu no Atosaki) (1931), trans. Lane Dunlap (Stanford, 1994)

——, *A Strange Tale from East of the River* (Bokuto Kidan) (1937), trans. Edward Seidensticker (Stanford, 1965)

Nijo, Lady, *Confessions of the Lady Nijo*, trans. Wilfred Whitehouse and Eizo Yanagisawa (Tokyo, 1974)

Norman, Henry, *The Real Japan* (New York, 1892)

Olsen, Donald, *The City as a Work of Art* (New Haven, 1986)

Pezeu-Massabau, J., *L'Agglomération de Tokyo* (Paris, 1974)

Pons, Philippe, *D'Edo à Tokyo* (Paris, 1988)

Popham, Peter, *Tokyo: The City at the End of the World* (Tokyo, 1985)

Quennell, Peter, *A Superficial Journey through Tokyo and Peking* (London, 1932)

Reid, Alastair, *Whereabouts: Notes on Being a Foreigner* (San Francisco, 1987)

Richie, Donald, *Introducing Tokyo* (Tokyo, 1987)

——, *A Lateral View* (Tokyo, 1991)

——, *Partial Views* (Tokyo, 1995)

——, 'Tokyo', *Orient-East*, 1/3 (1960)

——, 'Walking in Tokyo', in *Tokyo: Form & Spirit* (New York, 1986)

Riesman, David, *Conversations with Japan* (New York, 1967)

Rosenthal, A. M., and Arthur Gello, eds, *The Sophisticated Traveller* (New York, 1984)

Saïd, Edward, *Orientalism* (New York, 1978)

Sancton, Thomas, 'Tokyo: Inside the Super City', *Time*, 5 May 1986

Sarashina, [Lady], *As I Crossed the Bridge of Dreams* (Sarashina Nikki), trans. Ivan Morris (New York, 1971)

Seidensticker, Edward, *Kafu the Scribbler: The Life and Writings of Nagai Kafu, 1879–1959* (Stanford, 1965)

——, *Low City, High City: Tokyo from Edo to the Earthquake* (New York, 1983)

——, *Tokyo Rising* (New York, 1990)

Sennett, Richard, *Flesh and Stone: The Body and the City in Western Civilization* (New York, 1994)

Siebald, Phillipp Franz von, *Manners and Customs of the Japanese* (London, 1841; reprint Tokyo, 1973)

Singer, Kurt, *Mirror, Sword and Jewel* (London, 1973)

Smith, Henry D., II, *Edo-Tokyo Gaku Josetsu* (Tokyo, 1985)

Steffins, Lincoln, *Autobiography* (New York, 1931)

Taito Ward Board of Education, *The Shitamachi Museum* (Tokyo, 1983)

Takashina Shuji, ed., 'Tokyo: Creative Chaos', *Japan Echo*, XIV (1987) (special issue)

Tange Kenzo, 'Tokyo – Its Past and Future', *Japan Times*, 4–5 January 1987

Tanizaki Junichiro, *Childhood Years* (Yoshi Jidai) (1956), trans. Paul McCarthy (Tokyo, 1988)

——, *Diary of a Mad Old Man* (Futen Roji Nikki) (1962), trans. Howard Hibbett (New York, 1965)

——, *The Makioka Sisters* (Sasameyuki) (1944), trans. Edward Seidensticker (New York, 1957)

——, 'The Secret' (Himitsu) (1911), trans. Anthony Chambers in *New Leaves: Studies and Translations of Japanese Literature in Honor of Edward Seidensticker*, eds Aileen Gatten and Anthony Chambers (Ann Arbor, MI, 1993)

Teshigahara Hiroshi, 'An Ideal City', *So*, no. 128 (1988)

Thomson, J. Michael, *Great Cities and Their Traffic* (London, 1978)

Thwaite, Anthony, 'Tokyo, a Jumbled, Confused City', *Asahi Evening News*, 26 March 1986

Tokyo Metropolitan Government, *Tokyo Life*, xxx (1996)

Waley, Paul, *Tokyo: City of Stories* (Tokyo, 1991)

——, *Tokyo Now and Then* (Tokyo, 1984)

Ward, Philip, *Japanese Capitals* (Cambridge, 1985)

Yazaki Takeo, *The Japanese City* (Tokyo, 1963)